CW00919849

*Ae fond kiss*

'Clarinda's house, General's Entry'
(from *Old and New Edinburgh* by James Grant, 1882)

# THE LOVE LETTERS OF
# ROBERT BURNS AND CLARINDA

---

## EDITED BY DONNY O'ROURKE

MERCAT PRESS
EDINBURGH
*www.mercatpress.com*

First published in 2000 by Mercat Press
James Thin, 53 South Bridge, Edinburgh EH1 1YS
Based on *The Correspondence Between Burns and Clarinda* edited by
W.C. M'Lehose, published in 1843
© Donny O'Rourke, 2000

ISBN 184183 0186

Set in Aldine at Mercat Press
Printed and bound in Great Britain by Bell & Bain Ltd., Glasgow

# Contents

# Acknowledgements

Enthusiasm should not be mistaken for expertise. My interest in Burns has been deepened, quickened and learnedly surpassed by those real Burns experts, Ken Simpson, Gerry Carruthers and Andrew Noble. Ken Simpson's annual Burns conferences at Strathclyde University have been an inspiration to me, and hundreds of others. By putting its money where my mouth was, Glasgow City Council, for which I directed a year-long Burns Festival, enabled, indeed obliged me to do some more work on the bard in the company of many outstanding scholars and performers of Burns. Thanks to David Boyd and Catherine McInerney for all those rapt hours in the Mitchell Library's Burns Room. The last bits of work on this book were done when I was on the other side of the Atlantic, and I thank the staff at the library of the University of Chicago for their patience and persistence. It was Seán Costello who proposed and meticulously oversaw this project, and I am very grateful to him. And to Tom Wright, whose play *There Was A Man* did so much to reclaim and restore the real Robert Burns, I extend my thanks for his insights and friendship.

# Note on the Text

This book reproduces without abridging or amendment, the text published by William Tait of Edinburgh in 1843. Edited by W.C. M'Lehose, the grandson of Agnes (Nancy) M'Lehose—Clarinda, to the Sylvander of Robert Burns—the book contained most of the extant correspondence between the two, a memoir of Clarinda and the poems Burns and Mrs M'Lehose exchanged. Successful and frequently reprinted in its day, the book retains a great deal of fascination and poignancy as a product of that time. The letters were included in *Clarinda* by Raymond Lamont Brown (1968). Some readers, indeed many, we hope, will be surprised that the correspondence *per se* has been so long out of print. Although J. Delancey Fergusson's painstaking resequencing of the letters corrected the 1843 order here and there, as a record of this controversial relationship it is complete, except for letters destroyed, lost or withheld on grounds of taste or discretion by W.C. M'Lehose. We reprint three missing letters by Burns as an appendix here. W.C. M'Lehose's footnotes have been retained and new endnotes added.

Information about the disputed plaque to Clarinda was gleaned from John G. Gray and Charles J. Smith's *A Walk on the Southside in the Footsteps of Robert Burns* (1998).

The present edition in no way supersedes, indeed depends gratefully and admiringly on, collections of the complete letters of Robert Burns, edited and annotated by G. Ross Roy and James McKay respectively. Since the former adopts a chronological approach and the latter groups letters according to addressees, they can be seen to complement each other very well. By including the letters addressed to Burns by Clarinda, and by presenting the correspondence as a chronological epistolary narrative, the present edition aims to complement Roy and McKay in its turn. *Ae Fond Kiss* goes to press ahead of, and therefore without benefiting from, Dr Kenneth Simpson's forthcoming, much-needed and long-awaited study of the letters. Those wishing scholarly analysis and insight into these and other letters of Burns, will find definitive guidance there.

## FURTHER READING

Facts are chiels that winna ding and today we are, thanks to excellent recent biographies by James MacKay and Ian MacIntyre, in possession of them. Catherine Carswell's life of the poet reads like a Lawrentian novel and is still thrillingly revealing nearly seventy years after it was first published. David Daiches' study of the poet and the poems is masterly and unlikely to be bettered, as is Tom Crawford's book about the lyrics. Donald Low and Kirsteen McCue have done invaluable work on the songs and a complete recording is in progress from Linn Records to add to Jean Redpath's magnificent interpretations of Serge Hovey's arrangements. Carol McGuirk's Penguin *Selected Poems* has complemented James Kingsley's Oxford *Collected Poems*. On these (and many other) fine sources, I have drawn. Any errors are mine and mine alone. But I commend this selective reading list to anyone wishing to take their interest in the poet further.

# Biographical Note

Donny O'Rourke is a poet, journalist and broadcaster, and directs the Scottish Cultural Studies programme at the Glasgow School of Art. Formerly Head of Arts at Scottish Television and an executive producer at BBC Scotland, his many films and television programmes include several on Robert Burns, and he is in much demand both in Scotland and overseas as a speaker at Burns conferences and suppers. Among his publications are the anthology *Dream State: The New Scottish Poets* (1994), and *The Waistband & Other Poems* (1997).

# INTRODUCTION

The whole world loves a lover: Petrarch and Laura, Dante and Beatrice, Abelard and Eloise, Frank Sinatra and Ava Gardner... Robert Burns and Agnes M'Lehose? Don't smirk; Sylvander and Clarinda were never as starrily star-crossed as Romeo and Juliet, yet theirs is a love story to rank with the great ones, a *grand amour* in its way, an affair of enormous significance to the two lovers, and of considerable importance for us.

Burns was a letter writer to rank with Keats, Elizabeth Bishop or Simone de Beauvoir (whose airmail romance with Nelson Algren makes equally touching reading), a man almost incapable of penning a tiresome sentence—I say almost, because the missives to Mrs M'Lehose do contain longueurs. This was above all an epistolary intrigue and the letters to and from 'Nancy' cast fascinating light on the poet.

Francis Jeffrey believed that all Burns' letters were composed as 'exercises and for display'. He took pride in his flair for letter writing, always revising his drafts and making collections of his most successful efforts. In the absence of diaries, or descriptions by his fellow writers, his letters are our most important biographical source.

Agnes M'Lehose, however, pursues her own claim on posterity's attention. An interesting woman, rich in self-knowledge, she is not, to judge by the power of her pen, nearly so asinine a figure as she has been made out to be. From Allan Cunningham's time onwards (he applied unsuccessfully to publish the letters in 1834), the relationship between the newly lionised bard and the young grass widow has been portrayed as being gently risible. There have been innumerable references to hothouse romances, overheated platonic posturing and so on. They do make fools of themselves. With *noms d'amours* like Clarinda and Sylvander, how could they fail to? But love makes fools of us all. So Burns and his Nancy indulge in some epistolary dressing up; where's the harm? Remember Charles Windsor and those bizarre tampon phone calls to his married mistress?—he wishes we didn't. In the idea of the ploughman poet as Nancy's bit of rough and the kenspeckle hostess as his bit of fluff, there is some truth.

To read their correspondence straight through like a romantic novel is to encounter real feeling amid the attitudinising and twaddle. As the genre requires, this love story has an intriguing beginning, a suspenseful middle and an affectingly unhappy ending. Burns the songsmith even provides the perfect theme tune for that tear-jerking fade to black. In truth the whole scenario was powerfully cinematic *avant la lettre*. Now, it cries out for and looks likely to get the big-screen treatment for real.

Because the Clarinda/Sylvander correspondence (as a volume in its own right) has been so long out of print, few who sneer and snipe at its alleged vapidity and spurious pastoralism have had the chance to spend a sympathetic hour or two in the company of these questing, vulnerable, ardent souls. A self-consciously romantic romance before the idea of Romance had been invented (Nancy refers to Fielding's *Amelia*, Burns was rapidly turning into MacKenzie's 'Man Of Feeling'), this is romance nonetheless. Whether our taste runs to Bridget Jones' Mr Darcy or Jane Austen's or both, we will find plenty that is recognisable here.

Hyperbole frequently mars the correspondence so I will not exaggerate its qualities. The letters between Abelard and Eloise soar higher. Beauvoir's to Algren delve deeper. There, true love is heartbreakingly and precisely that. Burns' letters to Nancy do not always ring true. And nor, less often, do hers to him. But if they are sometimes strained and often pained, they have heat and heart as well as histrionic fatuousness. And besides, hothouse flowers have an extravagant lushness Scotland lacks.

———————

Many of the greatest love stories have the good taste and gumption to end badly and sadly. In the matter of Clarinda and Sylvander, no one expected or even wanted a happy ending, and this, one suspects, includes the protagonists themselves. Juliet plays dead. Romeo stays dead. Eighteenth-century bowdlerisers broke a law of nature by daring to suggest otherwise. *Brief Encounter* is unthinkable without, indeed is actually about, its snuffle-inducing finale. To be sure, this brief encounter ended sooner than Clarinda might have hoped. There were plenty more lyrics and love letters where those came from; amatory commonplaces bubbled out of Mrs M'Lehose like lava. Her beloved, however, behaved like a bounder. The relationship was going nowhere, but Burns was going to Dumfries, finally and predictably marrying the woman he had bad-mouthed to her rival. The rest is history: songs for Johnson and Thomson, the strains of Ellisland and the excise; yet more children to yet more mothers; dwindling wealth and health; just one more consummate poem— the masterpiece *Tam o' Shanter*; the man who had been born in the country retreating to the town, in common with so many Scots of that time; debt, despair, death. Then the suppers, the statues; secular sainthood, in fact.

Oh yes, we know what became of Burns. But whatever happened to Nancy? Not enough, one fears. She didn't die young. Surviving to a (really) ripe old age, she sought solace and diversion from her friends, continuing to have faith in God, reading, writing and enjoying pleasant strolls—a quiet life that got quieter as her hearing diminished and her friends died off. Her New Year's Day parties had been renowned but gradually those and other flurries into fashionable society dropped away until Burns' muse was just another little old Edinburgh lady in a city famous for them. Sir Walter Scott saw her at the home of her cousin, Lord Craig, when she had become 'old, charmless and devout'. In her diary on 6 December 1831 she wrote: 'This day I can never forget. Parted with Burns in the year 1791, never more to meet in this world.—Oh, may we meet in Heaven!'

In 1937 the Edinburgh Clarinda Burns Club proposed erecting a plaque on the site of her little house in the General's Entry. There was uproar. Was Clarinda of 'good enough character' to deserve douce Edinburgh's regard? Only after questions were asked in the House of Commons did a modest memorial go up.

Until almost the end her favourite walk was around Calton Hill. There's a folly there as grand, handsome and unfinished as her own. Not far from its beautifully useless columns is the monument Auld Reekie raised to the man she loved. Some soft summer evening when the gloaming lingers late and the last of the light's all lavender and lemon, amble up, or let your imagination climb the hill, and recalling the letters they exchanged, think of, or better quietly sing, the song Stevenson called the 'essence of all love tales':

I'll ne'er blame my partial fancy,
Naething could resist my Nancy
But to see her, was to love her;
Love but her, and love for ever.

If much reflex rubbish has been talked about the Sylvander/Clarinda affair, that is true about Burns' time in Edinburgh generally. Conventional wisdom suggests the capital came close to destroying the poet. The truth is much more complex. Would that the same could be said of the poetry the *literati* (their own term) coaxed out of their latest discovery. What direly duff stuff it is, almost virtuosically vapid at times. The 'Address to a Haggis' is the best thing from the Edinburgh period: not coincidentally, a poem in honest, supple Scots, as opposed to the plummy grandiloquence of, 'Edina, Scotia's darling seat' and other verses purged of what David Hume had called, 'Scotticisms'. Let it not be overlooked, however, that the 'Heaven-Taught Ploughman' had a good deal of help from Burns himself. Anticipating the arch and disingenuous posing of the letters to Clarinda, Burns, pausing only to stick some metaphorical straw in his ears, played the unschooled rustic to a tee. This act was lapped up as the well-read, if not well-bred, would-be literary lion anticipated it would be. A certain amount of intellectual and social insecurity did afflict the perennially prickly poet who was, after all, of peasant stock, with the ploughman's stoop and lack of college polish to prove it. All too sickeningly Scottish was the way Edinburgh took him up only to ding him down when his season in the sun was over. For so proud a man such salon symbiosis and the fact of his own sing-for-your-supper complicity in the parlour games of the gentry must have been hard to stomach. 'Only if you also invite the learned pig,' he had snarled in response to one opportunistic overture too many. They tired of the unlearned poet soon enough. In a matter of months, there was no further need to decline such invitations.

To Edinburgh, Burns had cause, nonetheless, to be grateful. If the Kilmarnock edition made his name, the Edinburgh edition made his fame. That edition is inscribed with the names of the great and good including, and especially, the members of the Caledonian Hunt. In Edinburgh he met protectors and sponsors whose patronage would take him the length and breadth of the country from one great house to another. Those song-collecting tours were launched from the capital. In the capital were the men who would publish the songs he memorised, made and mended. After his induction into the prestigious Masonic lodge of Canongate Kilwinning, all manner of influence was just a handshake away. Bishop Geddes was in Edinburgh too, and this urbane Catholic prelate was to be instrumental in establishing Burns' European reputation. For his powers of conversation, for his charisma and poetic prowess, Edinburgh was a test. A test he did not fail. A capital no longer in anything but name, yet a proto-Nationalist redoubt for that reason, full of ghosts from the good old days before the unions of crown and parliaments, Edinburgh was irresistible to Burns; and vice versa. In Edinburgh there were highborn hearts to set aflutter. Hearts like Clarinda's.

In just the way that present-day pop stars and bestselling authors take to the road with their latest wares, Robert Burns felt it incumbent upon himself to make personal appearances after the sell-out success that was *Poems, Chiefly in the Scottish Dialect*. There were no T-shirts proclaiming, 'Robert Burns: The Kilmarnock Edition Tour', but a promotional tour it most assuredly was.

Resting on its Enlightment laurels, this was a city all too conscious of the esteem in which its thinkers were held. For Voltaire, Edinburgh was where one sought instruction in every art, 'from gardening to philosophy'. In November 1786, the Athens of the North was enjoying, perhaps a little too somnolently, a lull between Hume and Scott. Into that hiatus Henry MacKenzie and others were determined to thrust Scotland's newest literary star, the overnight sensation that was Robert Burns. Later the poet would write an egalitarian song that made his attitude to 'yon birkie ca'd a lord', anthemically clear. Writing to his friend Gavin Hamilton on 7 December, however, he had Edinburgh at his feet, and he knew it:

> For my own affairs, I am in a fair way of becoming as eminent as Thomas à Kempis or John Bunyan; and you may expect henceforth to see my birthday inserted among the wonderful events… My Lord Glencairn and the Dean of Faculty Mr Henry Erskine, have taken me under their wing, and by all probability, I shall soon be the tenth Worthy, and the eighth Wise Man of the world.

Add to that the Duchess of Gordon's influential aegis, and Burns had the protection of an extraordinary trio. 'The man will be spoiled if he can spoil,' wrote Mrs Cockburn. Who could blame Burns for being tempted? His talented brother Gilbert never escaped from subsistence and subservience.

But Edinburgh was not to be his ruin. An old Ayrshire mentor, Professor Dugald Stewart, furnished Currie, Burns' first biographer, with this portrait of the poet amongst the capital's gentry:

> His manners were then, as they continued ever afterwards, simple, manly, and independent; strongly expressive of conscious genius and worth; but without anything that indicated forwardness, arrogance, or vanity. He took his share in conversation, but not more than belonged to him…

And Burns, who has left us hardly any 'Scotticisms' in his outpourings to Clarinda and, indeed, only one letter to anyone in Scots, the splendid letter to his travelling companion Willie Nicol—a masterpiece it should be said—played the cultural chameleon so well that Stewart could add: 'Nothing was more remarkable among his various attainments than the fluency, precision, and originality of his language when he spoke in company…' In Scots or English, this was a man servants would get out of their beds to listen to. For Maria Riddell, great as was the poetry, the talk was more impressive still:

> If others have climbed more successfully to the heights of Parnassus, none certainly outshone Burns in the charms—the sorcery I would almost call it—of fascinating conversation; the spontaneous eloquence of social argument, or the unstudied poignancy of brilliant repartee… I believe no man was ever more gifted with a larger portion of the *vivada vis animi*…

But to see him was to love *him*. The compelling conversationalist dominated dinner table and drawing room with a life force that was mesmeric, a magnetism the sixteen-year-old Walter Scott was never to forget:

> …the eye alone, I think, indicated the poetical character and temperament. It was large, and of a cast which glowed (I say literally glowed) when he spoke with feeling or interest. I never saw such another eye in a human being, though I have seen the most distinguished men of my time. His conversation expressed perfect self confidence but without the least intrusive forwardness…

That was an Ayrshire farmer at the Sciennes house of Adam Fergusson, one of the Enlightenment's brightest leading lights.

Melancholy and doubt were never really banished. Such aplomb took work. In letters to his friends Aitken and Greenfield, he confessed: 'Various concurring circumstances have raised my fame as a Poet to a height which I am absolutely certain I have not merits to support; and I look down into the future as I would into the bottomless pit,' and: 'Never did Saul's armour sit so heavy on David when going to encounter Goliath, as does the encumbering robe of public notice with which the friendship and patronage of some "names dear to fame", have invested in me…' Never willing to suffer fools gladly (or otherwise), especially if their brains were in inverse proportion to their privileges, Burns was doubtless a bit too familiar with their womenfolk, a bit too scathing with his ripostes. As a letter to that frankest of candid friends, Mrs Dunlop, makes clear, mostly he was his own man: 'I have the advice of some very judicious friends among the *literati* here, but with them, I sometimes find it necessary to claim the privilege of thinking for myself.' That musky, muscular independence will have been tinder to Clarinda's flame.

Just months before, the intricacies of his love life (or lives), his failure in the flax business and his difficulties in finding a publisher had made emigration a real possibility. Instead he had, on a borrowed pony, set out for the capital with an expanded second edition in view. Thanks to the skinflint and crooked Creech whom he had met through Edinburgh's Crochallan Fencibles, that edition came triumphantly out with Burns still playing the ploughboy to considerable effect and in the most blamelessly bland Augustan English:

> Thy daughters bright thy walks adorn
> Gay as the gilded summer sky
> Sweet as the dewy milk white thorn
> Dear as the raptured thrill of joy.

This is not good, but there was worse to come, much worse. In Edinburgh, for Edinburgh and because of Edinburgh, Burns penned a line as gruesome as any ever written—William McGonagall and Murray Lachlan Young notwithstanding. His theme is the Stuart succession:

> Tho something like moisture conglobes in my eye
> Let no one misdeem me disloyal
> A poor friendless wanderer may well claim a sigh
> Still more if that wand'rer were royal.

Not a dry eye in the house, right enough.

For Nancy M'Lehose, *née* Agnes Craig, it was much more than a case of love at first sight. Born in 1759, the same year as the poet, she was the daughter of a prosperous and highly respected Glasgow surgeon. She had fallen head over heels with the very idea of Burns before that fateful tea party at Miss Nimmo's. If Burns had not already existed, she may well have had to invent him. Suspecting Scotland's unofficial poet laureate of good looks and even better conversation, she pestered an introduction out of her no doubt just-as-smitten friend. Her suspicions were confirmed. Though lacking finesse (*because* lacking finesse), the Ayrshire prodigy had the rough-hewn allure of the Noble Savage then so much in fashion. This was the man who wore a wee French queue or pony tail, 'the only tied hair in the parish,' the man who sported a plaid of his own distinctive hue draped in his own distinctive fashion, the man leaden-tongued local lads engaged as 'blackfoot' to do their wooing for them. 'An hour in the dark with Rob is worth a lifetime with any other lad,' it was said. And that was before he topped poetry's hit parade.

In Edinburgh he discovered the additional aphrodisiac power of fame. Pulchritude is power too. As, for a man like Burns, is social standing. Young Nancy M'Lehose was just plumply pretty enough, just sufficient of a lady, to fancy her chances. Ever since he had composed 'The Lass o Ballochmyle' for Wilhelmina Alexander, who had spurned his gauche advances (but unbeknown to him cherished those scribbled lines until her dying day), the poet had been drawn to, confused by and sexually unsuccessful with women from the upper strata. Pert, self-confident wee Mrs M'Elhose had the coquette's shrewd instinct for flirtation. For the elaborate production she had in mind—an eclogue blending fantasy and reality, propriety and risk— she was auditioning the perfect leading man. Tea at her house was the bait. The poet made excuses and a show of hesitation, then gulped. Jealous James M'Lehose, that neglectful bully and boor, was away playing the drunken wastrel. At a time when divorce was very rare, Nancy had retreated, first to her father's house, and then to Edinburgh. The couple had been separated for years. 'Good riddance' was the unanimous reaction to M'Lehose's continued absence. Burns, by contrast, was all too present; present and incorrect with a reputation that had gone before him. What delicious dangers danced in those deep, dark eyes. Country matters for a country man like Robert Burns were relatively straightforward, and in eighteenth-century Edinburgh fleshly lusts were all too easily assuaged. Did it suit Burns, the aspiring Parnassian, *à la* Shenstone and MacKenzie, to play the swooning swain, for a wee while at least? Probably. One can't see this enthusiastic fornicator turning physical intimacy down, but his amatory campaign was to be characterised by a half-hearted, half-hoping kind of ecstatic sublimation. Having written a rhapsody, he became one. Naturally the mark would be overstepped a little, the overwrought Nancy wouldn't have it any other way. Though every movement in the romantic symphony that was Clarinda bore the marking *agitato*, this would be a passionate but chaste affair—tears before bedtime, and instead of bedtime.

If not quite the classic Scotsman on the make, Robert Burns was nonetheless a young man in a hurry. His trip to Edinburgh was a raid with a spot of tourism attached: get the cash and cachet and get out. For Nancy M'Lehose that long-anticipated commingling of souls was all the more affecting because it was destined to be transitory. And then, oh munificent gods, Burns walloped his knee clambering out of a carriage. Cupid's aim was never truer. Obliged to tarry, the poet would visit after all, and in the meantime he would write. Write!— oh, how he would write. It was as if the lovelorn little Glaswegian had died and gone to heaven, a hellenic heaven full of gambolling nymphs and trilling shepherds. Then again, as Burns revealed to his intimate friend, the sea captain Richard Brown, he was eager to frolic himself: '…I am at this moment ready to hang myself for a young Edin' widow, who has wit and beauty, more murderously fatal than the assassinating stiletto of the Sicilian Banditti, or the poisoned arrow of the savage African…' Not a widow quite, but as good as, except in the proprieties that would cramp her venery style. In happier days the flashy young solicitor James M'Lehose had literally monopolised her by buying up every seat in the coach that bore her away to school in Edinburgh, his first and last romantic or imaginative act. Married at eighteen, four times a mother in as many years, Agnes was too young and frivolous, even had her husband proven less of a parsimonious and possessive brute. Judging by the silhouette Burns had Miers make of her, Nancy was plump, matronly and coquettish. More than the full lips and *retroussé* nose and curled lashes beneath

her veil and ribbon, one suspects it was her ability to project pretti-
ness, her flirtatious verve, that attracted Burns:

> I can say with truth, Madam, that I never met with a person in my life
> whom I more anxiously wished to meet again than yourself. To-night
> I was to have had that very great pleasure,—I was intoxicated with the
> idea; but an unlucky fall from a coach has so bruised one of my knees
> that I can't stir my leg off the cushion. So, if I don't see you again, I
> shall not rest in my grave for chagrin. I was vexed to the soul I had not
> seen you sooner. I determined to cultivate your friendship with the
> enthusiasm of religion; but thus has Fortune ever served me.

This was the rakish Rab who had earlier boasted to his friend
James Smith about his seducer's skill with the quill. He was indeed,
'an old hawk at the sport'. And the finely plumed little bird duly
cheeped:

> To-night I had thought of fifty things to say to you: how unfortunate
> this prevention! Do not accuse Fortune: had I not known she was
> *blind* before, her ill usage of *you* had marked it sufficiently. However,
> she is a fickle old beldame, and I'd much rather be indebted to *nature*.
> You shall *not* leave town without seeing me, if I should come along
> with good Miss Nimmo, and call for you. I am determined to see
> you; and am ready to exclaim with Yorick, 'Tut! are we not all rela-
> tions?' We are, indeed, *strangers* in one sense—but of near kin in many
> respects: those 'nameless feelings' I perfectly comprehend, though
> the pen of a Locke could not define them.

The keynote was thus sounded. To the whole panoply of seducer's
tricks and tropes, Burns had persuasive access. Capable of being most
things to most women, courtship for Burns was performance, sexual
and otherwise:

> Beware a tongue that's smoothly hung;
>   A heart that warmly seems to feel;
> That feelin heart but acks a part,
>   'Tis rakish art in Rob Mossgiel.
> The frank address, the soft caress,
>   Are worse than poisoned darts of steel,
> The frank address, and politesse,
>   Are all finesse in Rob Mossgiel.

There was no real Robert Burns to stand up. He never achieved
his ambition of writing a play, but he was a consummate actor. Some-
how the pen-pals are both play-acting and themselves. As a love offering between master and pupil, poems have a particular potency. Nancy

sends some verses to Burns who replies: 'Your lines, I maintain it, are poetry, and good poetry; mine were, indeed, partly fiction, and partly a friendship which, had I been so blest as to have met with you *in time*, might have led me—God of love only knows where. Time is too short for ceremonies.' No aria of *Don Giovanni* is more adroit. The emotional temperature rises. Is that haar or steam? The wrist extended as convention requires is, equally formulaically and lightly, slapped:

> When I meet you, I must chide you for writing in your romantic style. Do you remember that she whom you address is a married woman? or, Jacob-like, would you wait seven years, and even then, perhaps, be disappointed, as he was? No; I know you better: you have too much of that impetuosity which generally accompanies noble minds. To be serious, most people would think, by your style, that you were writing to some vain, silly woman to make a fool of her—or worse.

Just so. Soon Burns, pathetically milking his injury, in a gamey oedipal parody of mummy's little soldier extending his wounded limb, so that it can be (metaphorically, but who knows?) kissed better, is swinging the lead: 'My limb now allows me to sit in some peace; to walk I have yet no prospect of, as I can't mark it to the ground.'

There, there... This is literally lame. The Dundas family was not so soft a touch. At about this time Burns sent the Solicitor-General a rather bad elegy on the demise of his father Lord Arniston and answer came there none—a slight which rankled for the remainder of Burns' life. Going by the grisly occasional verse the poet was cranking out for and about any toffs whose wallets caught his eye, the lawyer was evidently a pretty astute judge of a criminally cringeworthy Pindaric ode: 'Pale Scotia's recent wound I may deplore.' More than the wound was to be deplored. Apart from auditioning as Scotland's unofficial poet laureate, Burns was on the lookout for a living when the time came to hobble out of Edinburgh.

It might be expected that the Edinburgh Penny Post, which ran from nine till nine, was connecting Burns in the Old Town and Nancy in the New. But the opposite was the case. She lived in straitened, jeopardised gentility in the Potterrow off Nicolson Street on the Southside while her temporarily shilpit correspondent lodged in St James' Square. In 1787, Playfair's New Town was still being laid out. Since both dwelled within 'an English mile of the cross of Edinburgh', they had no trouble putting in their almost daily tuppenceworth. More than daily: on 14 February 1788 (a less romantically charged day then than now) Burns was fulminating against the 'dreadful negligence' of the penny post which had held up that day's first letter from Clarinda, a clarifying note he was panting to receive and which caused him to revise the sequence of the narrative developing in his head. Parting may be such sweet sorrow; but meetings don't always fuel an affair as effectively as absence. In their first month of epistolary billing and cooing their hearts did, indeed, grow fonder, since they managed to meet only once. That Burns had begun to pin certain hopes on all this gushing ink may be suggested by his commissioning of a brooch bearing his own likeness for his latest love to wear next to her heart. Plainly Burns was no stranger at the jewellers: 'set it just as you did the others you made for me', he instructed Francis Howden of Parliament Square; obviously, like the entire imbroglio with Clarinda, it was something of a rush job.

At this distance, the proportion of cynical rakery in such ploys is impossible to determine. As the exchange deepens in intimacy, admittedly with Clarinda divulging, caring and expecting more than Sylvander, certain themes begin to emerge. Always more than just conventionally religious, Nancy begins to fret about Burns' laxity as a Calvinist. Concerned about her 'cousin-german' Lord Craig's jealousy of the poet, she drops hints to Burns about her protector's more than merely familial feelings towards her. His slightly creepy desire to be a kissing cousin in the most literal sense is brilliantly handled in Robert Kemp's now unjustly neglected play of 1957, *The Other Dear Charmer*, a *tour de force* that would form the basis for a more than serviceable film and could stand revival as exemplary theatre. The playwright is magisterial in the squalid matter of Jenny Clow, Clarinda's servant, who succumbed where her mistress did not. Of course, there was issue—it wasn't just Burns' imagination that was unusually fertile. How must Clarinda have felt at these upstairs–downstairs shenanigans? 'Live? We have servants to do that for us.'? I think not. The religious and determinedly pure Clarinda would have felt jealousy, incomprehension, betrayal and hurt.

There is too, the running (or limping) gag about that nobbled knee. And, more seriously, Jean Armour comes in and out of focus as Burns dithers and swithers, telling each woman what he thinks she wishes to hear. Young Bob Ainslie enters the frame too. Was there a wee touch of rivalry between the old friends, with the other Robert silently reproaching Burns for being so callously cavalier? Ainslie remained a true friend to Clarinda long after Burns cleared off, long after the poet's death, in fact. For now Burns was piquing Nancy's interest with a bit of will-he-won't-he? tantalising suspense. Nowadays she would be kept waiting by the phone. Burns the director manages Burns the actor with ineffable panache. As I say, what a loss he was to a Scottish theatre, direly in need of such talents:

> You cannot imagine, Clarinda, (I like the idea of Arcadian names in a commerce of this kind,) how much store I have set by the hopes of your future friendship. I don't know if you have a just idea of my character, but I wish you to see me as *I am*. I am, as most people of my trade are, a strange Will-o'-wisp being; the victim, too frequently, of much imprudence, and many follies. My great constituent elements are pride and passion: the first I have endeavoured to humanize into integrity and honour; the last makes me a devotee, to the warmest degree of enthusiasm, in love, religion, or friendship: either of them, or altogether, as I happen to be inspired. 'Tis true I never saw you but once; but how much acquaintance did I form with you at that once!

Did Clarinda ever stand a chance of seeing him as he was? Sylvander was also Robert Ruisseaux, Rob Mossgiel and many another *nom de plume* or *guerre*—a case of multiple Burns.

By early 1788, economic push was coming to shove and Burns, for all his prickly pride, was having to do a bit of trawling and crawling in search of work. To Clarinda he mentioned a matter in hand which 'hurries me much'; this was the softening up of Graham of Fintry, the Excise Commissioner, in hopes of a situation as a gauger. With his mind on the exacting duties of a customs officer and the prospect of real toil in actual, far-from-idyllic fields, Burns was too preoccupied for pastoral posturing in the pastures of Arcady. He let slip his fondness for the one 'whose name is indelibly written in my heart's core'. To which late-night ramblings Nancy replied: 'take care lest virtue demand even friendship as a sacrifice'. Her bluff did not need to be called. Amends were made. Clarinda had taken to 'stalking' her wounded prey: 'I am probably to be in your Square this afternoon, near two o'clock. If your room be to the street, I shall have the pleasure of giving you a nod. I have paid the porter, and you may do so when you write. I'm sure they sometimes have made us pay double.

Adieu!' On 12 January Burns wrote twice (Clarinda's note which occasioned the second is lost):

> You talk of weeping, Clarinda: some involuntary drops wet your lines as I read them. Offend me, my dearest angel! You cannot offend me,—you never offended me. If you had ever given me the least shadow of offence, so pardon me my God as I forgive Clarinda. I have read yours again; it has blotted my paper. Though I find your letter has agitated me into a violent headache, I shall take a chair and be with you about eight.

A three-hanky letter! Just reading prose like this, one reaches for the smelling salts. The second coming! Obviously all was forgiven. The next day Clarinda had this to say:

> I will not deny it, Sylvander, last night was one of the most exquisite I ever experienced. Few such fall to the lot of mortals! Few, extremely few, are formed to relish such refined enjoyment. That it should be so, vindicates the wisdom of Heaven. But, though our enjoyment did not lead beyond the limits of virtue, yet today's reflections have not been altogether unmixed with regret. The idea of the pain it would have given, were it known to a friend to whom I am bound by the sacred ties of gratitude, (no more,) the opinion Sylvander may have formed from my unreservedness; and, above all, some secret misgivings that Heaven may not approve, situated as I am—these procured me a sleepless night; and, though at church, I am not at all well.
>
> Sylvander, you saw Clarinda last night, behind the scenes!

What brought on this attack of conscience? Concerns about her cousin and her minister Kemp? General propriety? A bout of petting, whether light or heavy? We do not know. If Catherine Carswell is right—and few believe she is—then consummation might have occurred at this point in the affair. It is hard to credit. Nancy is not the type. And although Burns is, he has a history of holding back when better-born love objects demand it. We are left to guess.

Once more, however, the epistolary church bells start to ring. Clarinda, worrying again about Burns' salvation, really does love him heart and *soul*. We may speculate that it was not the gospel that Burns had crossed Edinburgh to embrace… The shuttlecock is batted back:

> That you have faults, my Clarinda, I never doubted; but I knew not where they existed; and Saturday night made me more in the dark than ever. O, Clarinda! why would you wound my soul, by hinting

that last night must have lessened my opinion of you. True, I was behind the scenes with you; but what did I see? A bosom glowing with honour and benevolence; a mind ennobled by genius, informed and refined by education and reflection, and exalted by native religion, genuine as in the climes of Heaven; a heart formed for all the glorious meltings of friendship, love, and pity. These I saw. I saw the noblest immortal soul creation ever showed me.

Nancy was, it seems, not altogether averse to having him behind the scenes again:

Either to-morrow or Friday I shall be happy to see you. On Saturday, I am not sure of being alone, or at home. Say which you'll come? Come to tea if you please; but eight will be an hour less liable to intrusions. I hope you'll *come afoot*, even though you take a chair home. A chair is so uncommon a thing in our neighbourhood, it is apt to raise speculation—but they are all asleep by ten.

No change there then, the Glaswegian editor is tempted to point out! As Nancy's own poetic confidence develops she sends to Burns her engaging and perfectly competent lyric, 'To a Blackbird', for which Burns will select an air and include in the *Musical Museum*. A letter to Peggy Chalmers suggests that Burns, gripped by the blue devilment of depression, was reheating the old chestnut of a career in the army. He had plenty to be depressed about. To anxieties over Jean and the Excise were added his feelings of exasperation and betrayal concerning the cheat and chiseller Creech. Was it at this low moment that overblown but genuinely infatuated pastoral flummery turned into cynical pantomime, with Burns hollowly mugging, one jaundiced eye on the wings as he sought to make an almost excruciatingly hasty exit? On 24 January, Nancy had been once again flushed with conscience-stricken self-reproach.

Sylvander, the moment I waked this morning, I received a summons from Conscience to appear at the Bar of Reason. While I trembled before this sacred throne, I beheld a succession of figures pass before me in awful brightness! Religion, clad in a robe of light, stalked majestically along, her hair dishevelled, and in her hand the Scriptures of Truth, held open at these words—'If you love me, keep my commandments.' Reputation followed: her eyes darted indignation while she waved a beautiful wreath of laurel, intermixed with flowers, gathered by Modesty in the Bower of Peace. Consideration held her bright mirror close to my eyes, and made me start at my own image! Love alone appeared as counsel in my behalf.

Such quivering heights (and depths) had by now been reached, and so guiltily besotted was Nancy, that one suspects that an hour spent holding hands and staring into each others' enraptured eyes could have brought on the paroxysm of passion of which she is so ashamed. She is not ready, for all her protestations, to give up what another denomination calls the occasion of sin. In any case plausibility was Burns' *métier*:

> Clarinda, my life, you have wounded my soul. Can I think of your being unhappy, even though it be not described in your pathetic elegance of language, without being miserable? Clarinda, can I bear to be told from you that 'you will not see me to-morrow night—that you wish the hour of parting were come!' Do not let us impose on ourselves by sounds. If, in the moment of fond endearment and tender dalliance, I perhaps trespassed against the *letter* of Decorum's law, I appeal, even to you, whether I ever sinned, in the very least degree, against the *spirit* of her strictest statute? But why, my love, talk to me in such strong terms; every word of which cuts me to the very soul? You know a hint, the slightest signification of your wish, is to me a sacred command.
>
> Be reconciled, my angel, to your God, yourself, and me; and I pledge you Sylvander's honour—an oath, I daresay, you will trust without reserve, that you shall never more have reason to complain of his conduct. Now, my love, do not wound our next meeting with any averted looks or restrained caresses. I have marked the line of conduct—a line, I know, exactly to your taste—and which I will inviolably keep…

Ainslie is introduced but has sufficient tact to slink away, leaving the lovers to canoodle. The tongues and fingers of Kemp and Craig wag. Their charge listens but does not heed. Off to Miers' studio she goes. Sylvander is backing off stage and she knows it:

> Alas! I shudder at the idea of an hundred miles distance. You'll hardly write me once a-month, and other objects will weaken your affection for Clarinda. Yet I cannot believe so. Oh, let the scenes of Nature remind you of Clarinda! In winter, remember the dark shades of her fate; in summer, the warmth, the cordial warmth, of her friendship; in autumn, her glowing wishes to bestow plenty on all; and let spring animate you with hopes, that your friend may yet live to surmount the wintry blasts of life, and revive to taste a spring-time of happiness! At all events, Sylvander, the storms of life will quickly pass, and 'one unbounded spring encircle all.' There, Sylvander, I trust we'll meet. Love, there, is not a crime. I charge you to meet me there—Oh, God!—I must lay down my pen.

Doubtless Burns was hoping that she would! The minister and the protector grow more incensed, and one of them writes an admonitory letter to Nancy which she sends on to Burns, who fulminates against the 'puritanical scrawl'. We don't know which puritan produced the scrawl because several letters from this period are unaccounted for. After midnight Burns takes up his pen again, and twice more the next day:

> I am yours, Clarinda, for life. Never be discouraged at all this. Look forward: in a few weeks I shall be somewhere or other, out of the possibility of seeing you: till then, I shall write you often, but visit you seldom. Your fame, your welfare, your happiness, are dearer to me than any gratification whatever. Be comforted, my love! the present moment is the worst; the lenient hand of time is daily and hourly either lightening the burden, or making us insensible to the weight. None of these friends—I mean Mr —— and the other gentleman—can hurt your worldly support: and of their friendship, in a little time you will learn to be easy, and by and by to be happy without it. A decent means of livelihood in the world, an approving God, a peaceful conscience, and one firm trusty friend—can anybody that has these be said to be unhappy? These are yours.
>
> To-morrow evening I shall be with you about eight, probably for the last time till I return to Edinburgh.

Was he exaggerating here and screwing up his outrage to provide the excuse for a huffy, mock-reluctant retreat?

From the Black Bull Inn in Glasgow (now Marks and Spencer's Argyle Street store), Burns wrote to reassure, if not console, after dinner with his brother William and Richard Brown, the man who a few years before, in Irvine, had confirmed the poet in his vocation and was now about to embark for Grenada. The 'grace drink' the letter proposed will not have mollified much. From two or three letters a day, Clarinda was reduced to one a week:

> I wish you had given me a hint, my dear Sylvander, that you were to write me only once in a week. Yesterday I looked for a letter; to-day, never doubted it; but both days have terminated in disappointment. A thousand conjectures have conspired to make me most unhappy. Often have I suffered much disquiet from forming the idea of such an attention, on such and such an occasion, and experienced quite the reverse. But in you, and you alone, I have ever found my highest demands of kindness accomplished; nay, even my fondest wishes, not gratified only, but anticipated! To what, then, can I attribute your not writing me one line since Monday?

God forbid that your nervous ailment has incapacitated you for that office, from which you derived pleasure singly; as well as that most delicate of all enjoyments, pleasure reflected. To-morrow I shall hope to hear from you. Hope, blessed hope, thou balm of every wo, possess and fill my bosom with thy benign influence.

From Craig and Kemp, the moral heavies in this psychodrama, she had had a quantity of scolding, and her son's leg needed to be lanced (legs again). That she yearned for a cherishing word is obvious and one may be tempted to approve of Burns for offering the eighteenth-century equivalent of TLC.

If flattering one lover by disparaging another is ungallant, the terms in which Burns traduced the unflaggingly loyal and egregiously put-upon Jean go far beyond conduct unbecoming a gentleman. Between Burns as a bit of a lad and Burns as a bit of a cad, there is not much difference here: 'I called for a certain woman—I am disgusted with her; I cannot endure her… 'twas setting the expiring glimmer of a farthing taper beside the cloudless glory of the meridian sun. Here was tasteless insipidity, vulgarity of soul and mercenary fawning; I have done with her and she with me…' If he was trying to convince himself, he failed; if he was being cynically duplicitous, it is a squalid ploy. Soon he would, in 'O' A' the Airts', write for his 'farthing taper' a song lovelier than any of the florid hymns to the 'meridian sun':

> O' a' the airts the wind can blaw,
>   I dearly like the West;
> For there the bony Lassie lives,
>   The Lassie I lo'e best:
> There's wild-woods grow, and rivers row,
>   And mony a hill between;
> But day and night my fancy's flight
>   Is ever wi' my Jean.

For Richard Brown, at around the same time, he painted quite another picture, in which he towed Jean into 'convenient harbour'. This was Burns at his shitty, chauvinist worst. A little later that spring he furnished Ainslie with the notorious account of his reconciliation with Jean. '…I have f—d her til she rejoiced with joy unspeakable and full of glory… I swore her privately never to attempt any claim on me as a husband… Oh what a peacemaker is a guid weeliwilly pintle…' So much for nymphs and shepherds. Born alarmingly soon after this 'joy unspeakable', in some 'dry horse litter', both Jean's twin girls were dead within days of being delivered. Clarinda tried to put on a brave face, wishing Burns well with his scheme to farm on land of Patrick Miller's near Dumfries, but she was losing heart; and losing Burns. Sylvander at this point, as tireless with his pen as ever, is writing to everybody *except* Clarinda.

At last, or so it seemed to Clarinda, in the second week of March, Burns was back in an Edinburgh agog at the doings of the councillor-cum-burglar, Deacon Brodie, perhaps only slightly less villainous in the poet's eyes than the sly and intractable Creech. Burns' letters to Clarinda were augmented by several rendezvous that week. We don't have her replies to to his letters but the first faint notes of a finale were being struck up:

> Life, my Clarinda, is a weary, barren path; and wo be to him or her that ventures it alone! For me, I have my dearest partner of my soul: Clarinda and I will make out our pilgrimage together. Wherever I am, I shall constantly let her know how I go on, what I observe in the world around me, and what adventures I meet with. Will it please you, my love, to get, every week, or, at least, every fortnight, a packet, two or three sheets, full of remarks, nonsense, news, rhymes, and old songs?
>
> Will you open, with satisfaction and delight, a letter from a man who loves you, who has loved you, and who will love you to death, through death, and for ever?

On Monday at noon came the *coup de grâce*, a business-like note about his forthcoming induction into the Excise. As a keepsake Clarinda got a pair of drinking glasses. It says a lot for her that she didn't smash them, especially once she had read the verses that accompanied the farewell gift.

> Fair Empress of the Poet's soul,
> And Queen of Poetesses,
> Clarinda take this little boon,
> This humble pair of glasses.

You wouldn't have to be a queen of poetesses to apprehend just how insultingly maladroit this doggerel is. Did Burns the indefatigable rough wooer try one last time to present his determinedly innocent *inamorata* with rather a different gift? And was he rebuffed? On his way to talk customs business with Graham of Fintry (probably), he snatched a moment to fire off one last despatch referring to 'the evening rapture' and begging, 'Do not be uneasy today, Clarinda forgive me…' And that was that. Or very nearly.

Clarinda took the glasses down to show them off whenever she had the slightest excuse. On 9 March 1789, almost a year later, Sylvander wrote justifying himself and praising a woman whose friendship he guiltily hoped to retain. In 1791, she wrote to tell him about her own voyage to Jamaica on the selfsame *Roselle* he very nearly took. The soused and loutish M'Lehose let her down again. He would make and lose a fortune before dying of dissipation, no money having come Nancy's way. She wrote to inform the poet of Jenny Clow's death. He replied, acknowledging his guilt. For Burns she continued to 'carry a torch'. They 'kept in touch'. In company Burns would often raise a tipsy toast to 'Mrs Mac'. Muse of and touchstone for those good gone Edinburgh days, Clarinda will have come often to his mind with or without the aid of a dram. Nostalgia was always a prompt for Burns.

A little time and distance allowed the affair to inspire some really fine poetry at last. The best thing to come out of the whole episode by far, Clarinda's proper if belated parting gift from Burns, and a work of art in exchange for which he can be forgiven much, is the simple, yet ineffable lyric he set to the slow strathspey, 'Rory Dall's Port'. Though that original air is making a well-deserved comeback, the melody posterity preferred, the one we usually sing, brings its own atmosphere of gratitude and yearning to this sublime memorial to love and loss: but then Sylvander didn't write it; Burns did, and for Nancy, not Clarinda, true love after all:

> Ae fond kiss, and then we sever;
> Ae fareweel, alas, for ever!
> Deep in heart-wrung tears I'll pledge thee,
> Warring sighs and groans I'll wage thee.

# LETTER I

~

## SYLVANDER TO CLARINDA
### [*December 6, 1787.*]★

MADAM,—I had set no small store by my tea-drinking to-night, and have not often been so disappointed. Saturday evening I shall embrace the opportunity with the greatest pleasure. I leave this town this day se'ennight, and probably I shall not return for a couple of twelvemonths; but I must ever regret that I so lately got an acquaintance I shall ever highly esteem, and in whose welfare I shall ever be warmly interested. Our worthy common friend, Miss Nimmo,[1] in her usual pleasant way, rallied me a good deal on my new acquaintance; and, in the humour of her ideas, I wrote some lines, which I enclose you, as I think they have a good deal of poetic merit; and Miss Nimmo tells me that you are not only a critic but a poetess. Fiction, you know, is the native region of poetry; and I hope you will pardon my vanity in sending you the bagatelle as a tolerable off-hand *jeu d'esprit*. I have several poetic trifles, which I shall gladly leave with Miss Nimmo or you, if they were worth house room; as there are scarcely two people on earth by whom it would mortify me more to be forgotten, though at the distance of nine score miles.

I am, Madam,
With the highest respect,
Your very humble servant,
  BURNS.
*Thursday Even.*

———

# LETTER II

~

## SYLVANDER TO CLARINDA
### [*December 8.*]

I can say with truth, Madam, that I never met with a person in my life whom I more anxiously wished to meet again than yourself. To-night I was to have had that very great pleasure,—I was intoxicated with the idea; but an unlucky fall from a coach has so bruised one of

★Dates within brackets [ ] are given from the internal evidence of the letters, and some memoranda made in 1802 by Mrs M'Lehose's son.

my knees that I can't stir my leg off the cushion. So, if I don't see you again, I shall not rest in my grave for chagrin. I was vexed to the soul I had not seen you sooner. I determined to cultivate your friendship with the enthusiasm of religion; but thus has Fortune ever served me. I cannot bear the idea of leaving Edinburgh without seeing you. I know not how to account for it—I am strangely taken with some people, nor am I often mistaken. You are a stranger to me;—but I am an odd being. Some yet unnamed feelings—things, not principles, but better than whims—carry me farther than boasted reason ever did a philosopher.

Farewell! every happiness be yours.

ROBERT BURNS.

*Saturday Even., St James' Sqr., No. 2.*★

## LETTER III†

CLARINDA TO SYLVANDER
*Saturday Evening,* [*December 8th.*]

Inured as I have been to disappointments, I never felt more, nay, nor half so severely, for one of the same nature! The cruel cause, too, augments my uneasiness. I trust you'll soon recover it. Meantime, if my sympathy, my friendship, can alleviate your pain, be assured you possess them. I am much flattered at being a favourite of yours. Miss Nimmo can tell you how earnestly I had long pressed her to make us acquainted. I had a presentiment that we should derive pleasure from the society of each other. To-night I had thought of fifty things to say to you: how unfortunate this prevention! Do not accuse Fortune: had I not known she was *blind* before, her ill usage of *you* had marked it sufficiently. However, she is a fickle old beldame, and I'd much rather be indebted to *nature*. You shall *not* leave town without seeing me, if I should come along with good Miss Nimmo, and call

---

★Now No. 30, the south corner house of the west side of the Square.
†This is one of the few Letters of which the address has been preserved. It is addressed, "Mr Robert Burns, Mr Cruickshank's, James' Square." Mr Cruickshanks, with whom Burns stayed during his visit to Edinburgh, was one of the masters of the High School. The address on the letters which Clarinda wrote, have generally been obliterated with ink; while those she received have usually been cut or torn off—to gratify (it is supposed) autograph collectors. Sometimes several lines of writing on the previous page are thus lost.

for you. I am determined to see you; and am ready to exclaim with Yorick, "Tut! are we not all relations?" We are, indeed, *strangers* in one sense—but of near kin in many respects: those "nameless feelings" I perfectly comprehend, though the pen of a Locke could not define them. Perhaps *instinct* comes nearer their description than either "principles or whims." Think ye they have any connexion with that "heavenly light which leads astray?" One thing I know, that they have a powerful effect upon me; and are delightful when under the check of *reason* and *religion*.

Miss Nimmo was a favourite of mine from the first hour I met with her. There is a softness, a nameless something about her, that, were I a man, old as she is, I should have chosen her before most women I know. I fear, however, this liking is not *mutual*. I'll tell you why I think so, at meeting. She was in mere jest when she told you I was a poetess. I have often composed rhyme, (if not *reason*,) but never one line of *poetry*. The distinction is obvious to every one of the least discernment. Your lines were truly poetical: give me all you can spare. Not one living has a higher relish for poetry than I have; and my reading everything of the kind makes me a tolerable judge. Ten years ago such lines from such a hand would have half-turned my head. Perhaps you thought it might have done so even *yet*;—and wisely premised, that "*Fiction* was the native region of poetry." Read the enclosed, which I scrawled just after reading yours. Be sincere; and own that, whatever merit it has, it has not a line resembling poetry. Pardon any little freedoms I take with you: if they entertain a heavy hour, they have all the merit I intended. Will you let me know, now and then, how your leg is? If I were your *sister*, I would call and see you; but 'tis a censorious world this; and (in this sense) you and I are not of the world. Adieu. Keep up your heart, you will soon get well, and we shall meet—Farewell. God bless you. A. M.

## LETTER IV

### SYLVANDER TO CLARINDA
*[December 12.]*

I stretch a point, indeed, my dearest Madam, when I answer your card on the rack of my present agony. Your friendship, Madam! By heavens, I was never proud before. Your lines, I maintain it, are poetry, and good poetry; mine were, indeed, partly fiction, and partly a friendship which, had I been so blest as to have met with you *in time,* might have led me—God of love only knows where. Time is too short for ceremonies.

I swear solemnly, (in all the tenor of my former oath,) to remember you in all the pride and warmth of friendship until—I cease to be!

To-morrow, and every day, till I see you, you shall hear from me.

Farewell! May you enjoy a better night's repose than I am likely to have.

## LETTER V

<small>CLARINDA TO SYLVANDER</small>
*Sunday, Noon,* [*December 16.*]

Miss Nimmo and I had a long conversation last night. Little did I suspect that she was of the party. Gentle, sweet soul! She is accusing herself as the cause of your misfortune. It was in vain I rallied her upon such an excess of sensibility, (as I termed it.) She is lineally descended from "My Uncle Toby"; has hopes of the Devil, and would not hurt a fly. How could you tell me that you were in "agony"? I hope you would swallow laudanum, and procure some ease from sleep. I am glad to hear Mr Wood[2] attends you. He is a good soul, and a safe surgeon. I know him a little. Do as he bids, and I trust your leg will soon be quite well. When I meet you, I must chide you for writing in your romantic style. Do you remember that she whom you address is a married woman? or, Jacob-like, would you wait seven years, and even then, perhaps, be disappointed, as he was? No; I know you better: you have too much of that impetuosity which generally accompanies noble minds. To be serious, most people would think, by your style, that you were writing to some vain, silly woman to make a fool of her—or worse. I have too much vanity to ascribe it to the former motive, and too much charity to harbour an idea of the latter; and viewing it as the effusion of a benevolent heart upon meeting one somewhat similar to itself, I have promised you my friendship: it will be your own fault if I ever withdraw it. Would to God I had it in my power to give you some solid proofs of it! Were I the Duchess of Gordon,[3] you should be possessed of that independence which every generous mind pants after; but I fear she is "no Duchess at the heart." Obscure as I am (comparatively,) I enjoy all the necessaries of life as fully as I desire, and wish for wealth only to procure the "luxury of doing good."

My chief design in writing you to-day was to beg you would not write me often, lest the exertion should hurt you. Meantime, if my scrawls can amuse you in your confinement, you shall have them occasionally. I shall hear of you every day from my beloved Miss Nimmo. Do you know, the very first time I was in her house, most of our conversation was about a certain (lame) poet? I read her soul in her expressive countenance, and have been attached to her ever since. Adieu! Be patient. Take care of yourself. My best wishes attend you. A. M.

## LETTER VI

### Sylvander to Clarinda.
#### [*December 20.*]

Your last, my dear Madam, had the effect on me that Job's situation had on his friends, when "they sat down seven days and seven nights astonied, and spake not a word."—"Pay my addresses to a married woman!" I started as if I had seen the ghost of him I had injured: I recollected my expressions; some of them indeed were, in the law phrase, "habit and repute," which is being half guilty. I cannot positively say, Madam, whether my heart might not have gone astray a little; but I can declare, upon the honour of a poet, that the vagrant has wandered unknown to me. I have a pretty handsome troop of follies of my own; and like some other people's retinue, they are but undisciplined blackguards: but the luckless rascals have something of honour in them; they would not do a dishonest thing.

To meet with an unfortunate woman, amiable and young, deserted and widowed by those who were bound by every tie of duty, nature, and gratitude, to protect, comfort, and cherish her; add to all, when she is perhaps one of the first of lovely forms and noble minds, the mind, too, that hits one's taste as the joys of Heaven do a saint—should a vague infant idea, the natural child of imagination, thoughtlessly peep over the fence—were you, my friend, to sit in judgment, and the poor, airy straggler brought before you, trembling, self-condemned, with artless eyes, brimful of contrition, looking wistfully on its judge,—you could not, my dear Madam, condemn the hapless wretch to death "without benefit of clergy"?

I won't tell you what reply my heart made to your raillery of "seven years"; but I will give you what a brother of my trade says on the same allusion:—

> The Patriarch to gain a wife,
> Chaste, beautiful, and young,
> Served fourteen years a painful life,
> And never thought it long.
> Oh were you to reward such cares,
> And life so long would stay,
> Not fourteen but four hundred years
> Would seem but as one day![4]

I have written you this scrawl because I have nothing else to do, and you may sit down and find fault with it, if you have no better way of consuming your time; but finding fault with the vagaries of a poet's fancy is much such another business as Xerxes chastising the waves of Hellespont.

My limb now allows me to sit in some peace; to walk I have yet no prospect of, as I can't mark it to the ground.

I have just now looked over what I have written, and it is such a chaos of nonsense that I daresay you will throw it into the fire, and call me an idle, stupid fellow; but whatever you think of my brains, believe me to be, with the most sacred respect, and heartfelt esteem,

My dear Madam,
Your humble servant,
ROBERT BURNS.*

## LETTER VII

SYLVANDER TO CLARINDA
[*December 21st.*]

I beg your pardon, my dear "Clarinda," for the fragment scrawl I sent you yesterday. I really don't know what I wrote. A gentleman for whose character, abilities, and critical knowledge, I have the highest

---

*Between this and the ensuing letter there was probably one signed "Clarinda" for the first time, now lost.

veneration, called in just as I had begun the second sentence, and I would not make the porter wait. I read to my much-respected friend several of my own bagatelles and, among others, your lines, which I had copied out. He began some criticisms on them, as on the other pieces, when I informed him they were the work of a young lady in this town; which, I assure you, made him stare. My learned friend seriously protested, that he did not believe any young woman in Edinburgh was capable of such lines: and, if you know anything of Professor Gregory, you will neither doubt of his abilities nor his sincerity. I do love you, if possible, still better for having so fine a taste and turn for poesy. I have again gone wrong in my usual unguarded way; but you may erase the word, and put esteem, respect, or any other tame Dutch expression you please in its place. I believe there is no holding converse, or carrying on correspondence with an amiable woman, much less a *gloriously-amiable fine woman*, without some mixture of that delicious passion, whose most devoted slave I have, more than once, had the honour of being. But why be hurt or offended on that account? Can no honest man have a prepossession for a fine woman, but he must run his head against an intrigue? Take a little of the tender witchcraft of love, and add it to the generous, the honourable sentiments of manly friendship, and I know but one more delightful morsel, which few, few in any rank ever taste. Such a composition is like adding cream to strawberries: it not only gives the fruit a more elegant richness, but has a peculiar deliciousness of its own.

I enclose you a few lines I composed on a late melancholy occasion.[5] I will not give above five or six copies of it at all; and I would be hurt if any friend should give any copies without my consent.

You cannot imagine, Clarinda, (I like the idea of Arcadian names in a commerce of this kind,) how much store I have set by the hopes of your future friendship. I don't know if you have a just idea of my character, but I wish you to see me as *I am*. I am, as most people of my trade are, a strange Will-o'-wisp being; the victim, too frequently, of much imprudence, and many follies. My great constituent elements are pride and passion: the first I have endeavoured to humanize into integrity and honour; the last makes me a devotee, to the warmest degree of enthusiasm, in love, religion, or friendship: either of them, or altogether, as I happen to be inspired.

'Tis true I never saw you but once; but how much acquaintance did I form with you at that once! Do not think I flatter you, or have a design upon you, Clarinda: I have too much pride for the one, and too little cold contrivance for the other; but of all God's creatures I ever could approach in the beaten way of acquaintance, you struck me with the deepest, the strongest, the most permanent impression. I say the most permanent, because I know myself well, and how far I can promise either on my prepossessions or powers. Why are you unhappy?—and why are so many of our fellow-creatures, unworthy to belong to the same species with you, blest with all they can wish? You have a hand all-benevolent to give,—why were you denied the pleasure? You have a heart formed, gloriously formed, for all the most refined luxuries of love,—why was that heart ever wrung. O Clarinda! shall we not meet in a state, some yet unknown state of being, where the lavish hand of Plenty shall minister to the highest wish of Benevolence, and where the chill north-wind of Prudence shall never blow over the flowery fields of enjoyment? If we do not, man was made in vain! I deserved most of the unhappy hours that have lingered over my head; they were the wages of my labour. But what unprovoked demon, malignant as hell, stole upon the confidence of unmistrusting, busy fate, and dashed your cup of life with undeserved sorrow?

Let me know how long your stay will be out of town: I shall count the hours till you inform me of your return. Cursed etiquette forbids your seeing me just now; and so soon as I can walk I must bid Edinburgh adieu. Lord, why was I born to see misery which I cannot relieve, and to meet with friends whom I can't enjoy! I look back with the pangs of unavailing avarice on my loss in not knowing you sooner. All last winter,—these three months past,—what luxury of intercourse have I not lost! Perhaps, though, 'twas better for my peace. You see I am either above, or incapable of dissimulation. I believe it is want of that particular genius. I despise design, because I want either coolness or wisdom to be capable of it. I am interrupted. Adieu, my dear Clarinda!

SYLVANDER.
*Friday Evening.*

## LETTER VIII

~

CLARINDA TO SYLVANDER
*Friday Evening,* [*Dec.* 21.]

I go to the country early to-morrow morning, but will be home by Tuesday—sooner than I expected. I have not time to answer yours as it deserves; nor, had I the age of Methusahem, could I answer it in kind. I shall grow *vain*. Your praises were enough,—but those of a Dr Gregory[6] superadded! Take care: many a "glorious" woman has been undone by having her head turned. "Know you!" I know you far better than you do me. Like yourself, I am a bit of an enthusiast. In religion and friendship quite a bigot—perhaps I could be so in love too; but everything dear to me in heaven and earth forbids! This is my fixed principle; and the person who would dare to endeavour to remove it I would hold as my chief enemy. Like you, I am incapable of dissimulation; nor am I, as you suppose, unhappy. I have been unfortunate; but guilt alone could make me unhappy. Possessed of fine children,—competence,—fame,—friends, kind and attentive,—what a monster of ingratitude should I be in the eye of Heaven were I to style myself unhappy! True, I have met with scenes horrible to recollection—even at six years' distance; but adversity, my friend, is allowed to be the school of virtue. It oft confers that chastened softness which is unknown among the favourites of Fortune! Even a mind possessed of natural sensibility, without this, never feels that exquisite pleasure which nature has annexed to our sympathetic sorrows. Religion, the only refuge of the unfortunate, has been my balm in every woe. O! could I make her appear to you as she has done to me! Instead of ridiculing her tenets, you would fall down and worship her very semblance wherever you found it!

I will write you again at more leisure, and notice other parts of yours. I send you a simile upon a character I don't know if you are acquainted with. I am confounded at your admiring my hues. I shall begin to question your taste,—but Dr G.! When I am low-spirited (which I am at times) I shall think of this as a *restorative*.

Now for the simile:—

> The morning sun shines glorious and bright,
> And fills the heart with wonder and delight!
> He dazzles in meridian splendour seen,

Without a blackening cloud to intervene.
So, at a distance viewed, your genius bright,
Your wit, your flowing numbers give delight.
But, ah! when error's dark'ning clouds arise,
When passion's thunder, folly's lightning flies,
More safe we gaze, but admiration dies.
And as the tempting brightness snares the moth,
Sure ruin marks too near approach to both.

Good night; for Clarinda's "heavenly eyes" need the earthly aid of sleep.
Adieu.

CLARINDA

P.S.—I entreat you not to mention our corresponding to one on earth.
Though I've conscious innocence, my situation is a delicate one.

## LETTER IX

CLARINDA TO SYLVANDER
*January 1, 1788.*

Many happy returns of this day to you, my dear, pleasant friend!
May each revolving year find you *wiser and happier!* I embrace the
first spare hour to fulfil my promise; and begin with thanking you for
the enclosed lines—they are very pretty: I like the idea of personifying
the vices rising in the absence of *Justice.* It is a constant source of
refined pleasure, giving "to airy nothings a local habitation and a
name," which people of a luxuriant imagination only can enjoy. Yet,
to a mind of a benevolent turn, it is delightful to observe how equal
the distribution of happiness is among all ranks! If stupid people are
rendered incapable of tasting the refined pleasures of the intelligent
and feeling mind, they are likewise exempted from the thousand
distractions and disquietudes peculiar to sensibility.

I have been staying with a dear female friend, who has long been
an admirer of yours, and was once on the brink of meeting with you
in the house of a Mrs Bruce. She would have been a much better
*Clarinda.* She is comely, without being beautiful,—and has a large
share of sense, taste, and sensibility; added to all, a violent penchant
for poetry. If I ever have an opportunity, I shall make you and her
acquainted. No wonder Dr Gregory criticised my lines. I saw several defects in them myself; but had neither time nor patience (nor
ability, perhaps,) to correct them. The three last verses were longer

than the former; and in the conclusion, I saw a vile tautology which I could not get rid of. But you will not wonder when I tell you, that I am not only ignorant of every language except my own, but never so much as knew a syllable of the English grammar. If I ever write grammatically, 'tis through mere habit. I rejoice to hear of Dr Gregory being your particular friend. Though unacquainted, I am no stranger to his character: where worth unites with abilities, it commands our love as well as admiration. Alas! they are too seldom found in one character! Those possessed of great talents would do well to remember, that all depends upon the use made of them. Shining abilities improperly applied, only serve to accelerate our destruction in both worlds. I loved you, for your fine taste in poetry, long before I saw you; so shall not trouble myself erasing the same word applied in the same way to me. You say, "there is no corresponding with an agreeable woman without a mixture of the tender passion." I believe there is no friendship between people of sentiment and of different sexes, without a *little* softness; but when kept within proper bounds, it only serves to give a higher relish to such intercourse. Love and Friendship are names in every one's mouth; but few, extremely few, understand their meaning. Love (or affection) cannot be genuine if it hesitate a moment to sacrifice every selfish gratification to the happiness of its object. On the contrary, when it would purchase that at the expense of this, it deserves to be styled, not love, but by a name too gross to mention. Therefore, I contend, that an honest man *may* have a friendly prepossession for a woman whose soul would abhor the idea of an intrigue with her. These are my sentiments upon this subject: I hope they correspond with yours. 'Tis honest in you to wish me to see you "just as you are." I believe I have a tolerably just idea of your character. No wonder; for had I been a man, I should have been you. I am not vain enough to think myself equal in abilities; but I am formed with a liveliness of fancy, and a strength of passion little inferior. Situation and circumstances have, however, had the effects upon each of us which might be expected. Misfortune has wonderfully contributed to subdue the keenness of my passions, while success and adulation have served to nourish and inflame yours. Both of us are incapable of deceit, because we want coolness and command of our feelings. Art is what I never could attain to, even in situations where a little would have been prudent. Now and then, I am favoured with a salutary blast of "the north wind of Prudence." The southern zephyrs of Kindness, too, often send up their sultry fogs, and cloud the atmosphere of my understanding. I have thought that "Nature" threw me off in the same mould, just after you. We were born, I believe, in one year. Madam Nature has some merit by her work that year. Don't you think so? I suppose the carline has had a flying visit of Venus and the Graces; and Minerva has been jealous of her attention, and sent Apollo with his harp to charm them away.

But why do you accuse Fate for my misfortunes? There is a noble independence of mind which I do admire; but, when not checked by religion, it is apt to degenerate into a criminal arraignment of Providence. No "malignant demon," as you suppose, was "permitted to dash my cup of life with sorrow:" it was the kindness of a wise and tender Father, who foresaw that I needed chastisement ore I could be brought to himself. Ah, my friend, Religion converts our heaviest misfortunes into blessings! I feel it to be so. These passions, naturally too violent for my peace, have been broken and moderated by adversity; and if even that has been unable to conquer my vivacity, what lengths might I not have gone, had I been permitted to glide along in the sunshine of prosperity? I should have forgot my future destination, and fixed my happiness on the fleeting shadows below! My hand was denied the bliss of giving, but Heaven accepts of the wish. My heart was formed for love, and I desire to devote it to Him who is the source of love! Yes: we shall surely meet in an "unknown state of being," where there will be full scope for every kind, heartfelt affection—love without alloy, and without end. Your paragraph upon this made the tears flow down my face! I will not tell you the reflections which it raised in my mind; but I wished that a heart susceptible of such a sentiment took more pains about its accomplishment. I fancy you will not wish me to write again; you'll think me too serious and grave. I know not how I have been led to be so; but I make no excuse, because I must be allowed to write to you as I feel, or not at all. You say you have humanized pride into "honour and integrity." 'Tis a good endeavour; and could you command your too-impetuous passions, it would be a more glorious achievement than his who conquered the world, and wept because he had no more worlds to subdue. Forgive my freedom with you: I never trouble myself with the faults of those I don't esteem, and only notice those of friends to themselves. I am pleased with friends when they tell me mine, and look upon it as a test of real friendship.

I have your poems in loan just now. I've read them many times, and with new pleasure. Sometime I shall give you my opinion upon them severally. Let me have a sight of some of your "Bagatelles," as you style them. If ever I write any more, you shall have them; and I'll thank you to correct their errors. I wrote lines on Bishop G.,[7] by way of blank verse; but they were what Pope describes—"Ten low words do creep in one dull line." I believe you (being a genius) have inspired me; for I never wrote so well before. Pray, is Dr Gregory pious? I have heard so. I wish I knew him. Adieu! You have quantity enough! whatever be the quality. Good night. Believe me your sincere friend,

CLARINDA

## LETTER X

CLARINDA TO SYLVANDER
*Thursday, Jan. [3d] 1788.*

I got your lines: they are "in *kind!*" I can't but laugh at my presumption in pretending to send my poor ones to *you!* but it was to amuse myself. At this season, when others are joyous, I am the reverse. I have no *near* relations and while others are with theirs, I sit alone, musing upon several of mine with whom I used to be—now gone to the land of forgetfulness.

You have put me in a rhyming humour. The moment I read yours, I wrote the following lines—

> Talk not of Love! it gives me pain—
> For Love has been my foe:
> He bound me in an iron chain
> And plunged me deep in woe

> But Friendship's pure and lasting joys
> My heart was form'd to prove—
> The worthy object be of those,
> But never talk of Love.

> The "Hand of Friendship" I accept—
> May Honour be our guard!

*Virtue* our intercourse direct,
  Her smiles our dear reward!★

But I wish to know (in sober prose) how your leg is? I would have inquired sooner had I known it would have been acceptable. Miss N. informs me now and then; but I have not seen her dear face for some time. Do you think you could venture this length in a coach, without hurting yourself? I go out of town the beginning of the week, for a few days. I wish you could come tomorrow or Saturday. I long for a conversation with you, and lameness of body won't hinder that. 'Tis really curious—so much *fun* passing between two persons who saw one another only *once!* Say if you think you dare venture;—only let the coachman be "adorned with sobriety."

Adieu! Believe me, (on my simple word,)

Your real friend and well-wisher,

A.M.

## LETTER XI

### SYLVANDER TO CLARINDA
*[January 3d.]*

MY DEAR CLARINDA,—Your last verses have so delighted me, that I have copied them in among some of my own most valued pieces, which I keep sacred for my own use. Do let me have a few now and then.

Did you, Madam, know what I feel when you talk of your sorrows!

Good God! that one, who has so much worth in the sight of heaven, and is so amiable to her fellow-creatures, should be so un-happy! I can't venture out for cold. My limb is vastly better; but I have not any use of it without my crutches. Monday, for the first time, I dine in a neighbour's, next door. As soon as I can go so far, *even in a coach*, my first visit shall be to you. Write me when you leave town, and immediately when you return; and I earnestly pray your

★The following stanza was afterwards added by Clarinda at the Poet's suggestion; it is here added from the original MS. in her own hand:

Your thought, if Love must harbour there,
  Conceal it in that thought,
Nor cause me from my bosom tear
  The very friend I sought.

stay may be short. You can't imagine how miserable you made me when you hinted to me not to write.

Farewell. Sylvander

## LETTER XII

Sylvander to Clarinda
*[January 4th.]*

You are right, my dear Clarinda; a friendly correspondence goes for nothing, except one write their undisguised sentiments. Yours please me for their intrinsic merit, as well as because they are yours; which, I assure you, is to me a high recommendation. Your religious sentiments, Madam, I revere. If you have, on some suspicious evidence, from some lying oracle, learnt that I despise or ridicule so sacredly-important a matter as real religion, you have, my Clarinda, much misconstrued your friend. "I am not mad, most noble Festus!" Have you ever met a perfect character? Do we not sometimes rather exchange faults than get rid of them? For instance, I am perhaps tired with and shocked at a life too much the prey of giddy inconsistencies and thoughtless follies. By degrees I grow sober, prudent, and statedly pious. I say statedly; because the most unaffected devotion is not at all inconsistent with my first character. I join the world in congratulating myself on the happy change. But let me pry more narrowly into this affair. Have I at bottom anything of a secret pride in these endowments and emendations? Have I nothing of a Presbyterian sourness, a hypercritical severity, when I survey my less regular neighbours? In a word, have I missed all those nameless and numberless modifications of indistinct selfishness which are so near our own eyes, that we can scarce bring them within our sphere of vision, and which the known spotless cambric of our character hides from the ordinary observer?

My definition of worth is short: truth and humanity respecting our fellow-creatures; reverence and humility in the presence of that Being, my Creator and Preserver, and who, I have every reason to believe, will one day be my Judge. The first part of my definition is the creature of unbiassed instinct; the last is the child of after reflection. Where I found those two essentials, I would gently note and slightly mention any attendant flaws—flaws, the marks, the consequences of human nature.

15

I can easily enter into the sublime pleasures that your strong imagination and keen sensibility must derive from religion, particularly if a little in the shade of misfortune; but I own I cannot, without a marked grudge, see Heaven totally engross so amiable, so charming a woman as my friend Clarinda; and should be very well pleased at *a circumstance* that would put it in the power of somebody, happy somebody! to divide her attention, with all the delicacy and tenderness of an earthly attachment.

You will not easily persuade me that you have not a grammatical knowledge of the English language. So far from being inaccurate, you are elegant beyond any woman of my acquaintance, except one, whom I wish you knew.

Your last verses to me have so delighted me, that I have got an excellent old Scots air that suits the measure, and you shall see them in print in the "*Scots Musical Museum*"[8]—a work publishing by a friend of mine in this town. I want four stanzas; you gave me but three, and one of them alluded to an expression in my former letter: so I have taken your two first verses, with a slight alteration in the second,— and have added a third—but you must help me to a fourth. Here they are: the latter half of the first stanza would have been worthy of Sappho. I am in raptures with it.

> Talk not of Love! it gives me pain—
> For Love has been my foe:
> He bound me with an iron chain,
> And sunk me deep in woe.
>
> But Friendship's pure and lasting joys
> My heart was form'd to prove:
> There, welcome win and wear the prize,
> But never talk of Love.
>
> Your friendship much can make me blest,
> O, why that bliss destroy?
> Why urge the odious★ one request,
> You know I must† deny?

The alteration in the second stanza is no improvement; but there was a slight inaccuracy in your rhyme. The third I only offer to your choice, and have left two words for your determination. The air is "The Banks of Spey," and is most beautiful.

★Var. "only."  †Var. "will."

To-morrow evening I intend taking a chair, and paying a visit at Park Place, to a much valued old friend. If I could be sure of finding you at home, (and I will send one of the chairmen to call,) I would spend from five to six o'clock with you, as I go past. I cannot do more at this time, as I have something on my hand that hurries me much. I propose giving you the first call, my old friend the second, and Miss Nimmo as I return home. Do not break any engagement for me, as I will spend another evening with you at any rate before I leave town. Do not tell me that you are pleased when your friends inform you of your faults. I am ignorant what they are; but I am sure they must be such evanescent trifles, compared with your personal and mental accomplishments, that I would despise the ungenerous, narrow soul, who would notice any shadow of imperfections you may seem to have, any other way than in the most delicate agreeable raillery. Coarse minds are not aware how much they injure the keenly feeling tie of bosom-friendship, when in their foolish officiousness they mention what nobody cares for recollecting. People of nice sensibility and generous minds have a certain intrinsic dignity, that fires at being trifled with, or lowered, or even too nearly approached.

You need make no apology for long letters: I am even with you. Many happy New Years to you, charming Clarinda! I can't dissemble, were it to shun perdition. He who sees you as I have done, and does not love you, deserves to be damned for his stupidity! He who loves you and would injure you, deserves to be doubly damned for his villany! Adieu.

SYLVANDER.

P.S.—.What would you think of this for a fourth stanza?*

---

*The lines which followed have been torn off the original MS.

## LETTER XIII

~

SYLVANDER TO CLARINDA
*[January 5th.]*

Some days, some nights, nay, some *hours*, like the "ten righteous persons in Sodom," save the rest of the vapid, tiresome, miserable months and years of life. One of these *hours* my dear Clarinda blest me with yesternight.

> —One well-spent hour,
> In such a tender circumstance for friends,
> Is better than an age of common time!
> THOMSON.

My favourite feature in Milton's Satan is his manly fortitude in supporting what cannot be remedied,—in short, the wild broken fragments of a noble exalted mind in ruins. I meant no more by saying he was a favourite hero of mine.

I mentioned to you my letter to Dr Moore,[9] giving an account of my life; it is truth, every word of it; and will give you the just idea of a man whom you have honoured with your friendship. I am afraid you will hardly be able to make sense of so torn a piece. Your verses I shall muse on—deliciously—as I gaze on your image, in my mind's eye, in my heart's core: they will be in time enough for a week to come. I am truly happy your headache is better. O, how can pain or evil be so daringly, unfeelingly, cruelly savage, as to wound so noble a mind, so lovely a form!

My little fellow is all my namesake.★ Write me soon. My every, strongest good wish attend you, Clarinda!

SYLVANDER.

*Saturday, Noon.*

I know not what I have written. I am pestered with people around me.

⟵——————⟶

---

★This was one of the twins born in 1786, and the eldest of the Poet's family. He was, long after his father's death, placed in the Stamp Office in London by Lord Sidmouth; from the duties of which he retired some years ago, and now resides in Dumfriesshire.

## LETTER XIV

CLARINDA TO SYLVANDER
*Monday Night, [January 7th.]*

I cannot delay thanking you for the packet of Saturday; twice have I read it with close attention. Some parts of it did beguile me of my tears. With Desdemona, I felt—"'twas pitiful, 'twas wond'rous pitiful." When I reached the paragraph where Lord Glencairn is mentioned, I burst out into tears. 'Twas that delightful swell of the heart which arises from a combination of the most pleasurable feelings. Nothing is so binding to a generous mind as placing confidence in it. I have ever felt it so. You seem to have known this feature in my character intuitively; and, therefore, intrusted me with all your faults and follies. The description of your first love-scene delighted me. It recalled the idea of some tender circumstances which happened to myself, at the same period of life—only mine did not go so far. Perhaps, in return, I'll tell you the particulars when we meet. Ah, my friend! our early love emotions are surely the most exquisite. In riper years we may acquire more knowledge, sentiment, &c.; but none of these can yield such rapture as the dear delusions of heart-throbbing youth! Like yours, mine was a rural scene, too, which adds much to the tender meeting. But no more of these recollections.

One thing alone hurt me, though I regretted many—your avowal of being an enemy to Calvinism. I guessed it was so by some of your pieces; but the confirmation of it gave me a shock I could only have felt for one I was interested in. You will not wonder at this, when I inform you that I am a strict Calvinist, *one or two* dark tenets excepted, which I never meddle with. Like many others, you are so, either from never having examined it with candour and impartiality, or from having unfortunately met with weak professors, who did not understand it; and hypocritical ones, who made it a cloak for their knavery. Both of these, I am aware, abound in country life; nor am I surprised at their having had this effect upon your more enlightened understanding. I fear your friend, the captain of the ship, was of no advantage to you in this and many other respects.

My dear Sylvander, I flatter myself you have some opinion of Clarinda's understanding. Her belief in Calvinism is not (as you will be apt to suppose) the prejudice of education. I was bred by my father in the Arminian principles. My mother, who was an angel, died when I was in my tenth year. She was a Calvinist,—was adored in her life,—and died triumphing in the prospect of immortality. I was too young, at that period, to know the difference; but her pious precepts and example often recurred to my mind amidst the giddiness and adulation of Miss in her teens. 'Twas since I came to this town, five years ago, that I imbibed my present principles. They were those of a dear, valued friend, in whose judgment and integrity I had entire confidence. I listened often to him, with delight, upon the subject. My mind was docile and open to conviction. I resolved to investigate, with deep attention, that scheme of doctrine which had such happy effects upon him. Conviction of understanding, and peace of mind, were the happy consequences. Thus have I given you a true account of my faith. I trust my practice will ever correspond. Were I to narrate my past life as honestly as you have done, you would soon be convinced that neither of us could hope to be justified by our good works.

If you have time and inclination, I should wish to hear your chief objections to Calvinism. They have been often confuted by men of great minds and exemplary lives,—but perhaps you never inquired into these. Ah, Sylvander! Heaven has not endowed you with such uncommon powers of mind to employ them in the manner you have done. This long, serious subject will, I know, have one of *three* effects: either to make you laugh in derision—yawn in supine indifference—or set about examining the hitherto-despised subject. Judge of the interest Clarinda takes in you when she affirms, that there are but few events could take place that would afford her the heartfelt pleasure of the latter.

Read this letter attentively, and answer me at leisure. Do not be frightened at its gravity,—believe me, I can be as lively as you please. Though I wish Madam Minerva for my guide, I shall not be hindered from rambling sometimes in the fields of Fancy. I must tell you that I admire your narrative, in point of composition, beyond all your other productions.—One thing I am afraid of; there is not a trace of friendship towards a female: now, in the case of Clarinda, this is the only "consummation devoutly to be wished."

You told me you never had met with a woman who could love as ardently as yourself. I believe it; and would advise you never to tie yourself, till you meet with such a one. Alas you'll find many who *canna*, and some who *manna*; but to be joined to one of the former description would make you miserable. I think you had almost best resolve against wedlock for unless a woman were qualified for the companion, the friend, and the mistress, she would not do for you. The last may gain Sylvander, but the others alone can keep him. Sleep, and want of room, prevent my explaining myself upon "infidelity in a husband," which made you stare at me. This, and other things, shall be matter for another letter, if you are not wishing this to be the last. If agreeable to you, I'll keep the narrative till we meet. Adieu! "Charming Clarinda" must e'en resign herself to the arms of Morpheus.

Your true friend,
CLARINDA.

*PS.*—Don't detain the porter. Write when convenient.

I am probably to be in your Square this afternoon, near two o'clock. If your room be to the street, I shall have the pleasure of giving you a nod. I have paid the porter, and you may do so when you write. I'm sure they sometimes have made us pay double. Adieu!

*Tuesday Morning.*

## LETTER XV

SYLVANDER TO CLARINDA
*[January 8th.]*

I am delighted, charming Clarinda, with your honest enthusiasm for religion. Those of either sex, but particularly the female, who are lukewarm in that most important of all things, "O my soul, come not thou into their secrets!"

I feel myself deeply interested in your good opinion, and will lay before you the outlines of my belief:—He who is our Author and Preserver, and will one day be our Judge, must be,—not for his sake, in the way of duty, but from the native impulse of our hearts,—the object of our reverential awe and grateful adoration. He is almighty and all-bounteous; we are weak and dependent: hence prayer and every other sort of devotion. "He is not willing that any should perish, but that all should come to everlasting life": consequently, it must be in every one's power to embrace His offer of "everlasting life"; otherwise he could not in justice condemn those who did not. A mind pervaded, actuated, and governed by purity, truth, and charity, though it does not *merit* heaven, yet is an absolutely-necessary prerequisite, without which heaven can neither be obtained nor enjoyed; and, by Divine promise, such a mind shall never fail of attaining "everlasting life": hence the impure, the deceiving, and the uncharitable exclude themselves from eternal bliss, by their unfitness for enjoying it. The Supreme Being has put the immediate administration of all this—for wise and good ends known to himself—into the hands of Jesus Christ, a great Personage, whose relation to Him we cannot comprehend, but whose relation to us is a Guide and Saviour; and who, except for our own obstinacy and misconduct, will bring us all, through various ways and by various means, to bliss at last.

These are my tenets, my lovely friend; and which, I think, cannot be well disputed. My creed is pretty nearly expressed in the last clause of Jamie Dean's grace, an honest weaver in Ayrshire:—"Lord, grant that we may lead a gude life! for a gude life maks a gude end: at least it helps weel."

I am flattered by the entertainment you tell me you have found in my packet. You see me as I have been, you know me as I am, and may guess at what I am likely to be. I, too, may say, "Talk not of Love," &c.; for, indeed, he has "plunged me deep in woe!" Not that I ever saw a woman who pleased unexceptionably, as my Clarinda elegantly says, "in the companion, the friend, and the mistress." *One*, indeed, I could except; one, before passion threw its mists over my discernment, I knew,—the first of women! Her name is indelibly written in my heart's core; but I dare not look in on it,—a degree of agony would be the consequence. Oh, thou perfidious, cruel, mischief-making demon, who presidest o'er that frantic passion,—thou mayest, thou dost poison my peace, but shalt not taint my honour! I would not for a single moment give an asylum to the most distant imagination that would shadow the faintest outline of a selfish gratification at the expense of *her*, whose happiness is twisted with the threads of my existence. May she be happy, as she deserves! And if my tenderest, faithfulest friendship can add to her bliss, I shall, at least, have one solid mine of enjoyment in my bosom! *Don't guess at these ravings!*

I watched at our front window to-day, but was disappointed. It has been a day of disappointments. I am just risen from a two-hours' bout after supper, with silly or sordid souls who could relish nothing in common with me but the Port. "One! "—'Tis now the "witching time of night," and whatever is out of joint in the foregoing scrawl, impute it to enchantments and spells; for I can't look over it, but will seal it up directly, as I don't care for to-morrow's criticisms on it.

You are by this time fast asleep, Clarinda; may good angels attend and guard you as constantly and as faithfully as my good wishes do!

> Beauty which, whether waking or asleep,
> Shot forth peculiar graces.

John Milton, I wish thy soul better rest than I expect on my pillow to-night! O for a little of the cart-horse part of human nature! Good night, my dearest Clarinda!

SYLVANDER.
*Tuesday Night.*

## LETTER XVI

CLARINDA TO SYLVANDER
*Wednesday, 10 P.M., [ January 9th.]*

This moment your letter was delivered to me. My boys are asleep. The youngest has been for some time in a crazy state of health, but has been worse these two days past. Partly this and the badness of the day prevented my exchanging a heartfelt How d'ye, yesterday. Friday, if nothing prevents, I shall have that pleasure, about two o'clock, or a little before it.

I wonder how you could write so distinctly after two or three hours over a bottle; but they were not congenial whom you sat with, and therefore your spirits remained unexhausted; and when quit of them, you fled to a friend who can relish most things in common with you (except Port.) 'Tis dreadful what a variety of these "silly, sordid" souls one meets with in life! but in scenes of mere sociability these pass. In reading the account you give of your inveterate turn for social pleasure, I smiled at its resemblance to my own. It is so great, that I often think I had been a man but for some mistake of Nature. If you *saw* me in a merry party, you would suppose me only an enthusiast in *fun*; but I now avoid such parties. My spirits are sunk for days after; and, what is worse, there are sometimes dull or malicious souls who censure me loudly for what their sluggish natures cannot comprehend. Were I possessed of an independent fortune, I would scorn their pitiful remarks; but everything in my situation renders prudence necessary.

I have slept little these two nights. My child was uneasy, and that kept me awake watching him! Sylvander, if I have merit in anything, 'tis in an unremitting attention to my two children; but it cannot be denominated merit, since 'tis as much inclination as duty. A prudent woman (as the world goes) told me she was surprised I loved them, "considering what a father they had." I replied with acrimony, I could not but love my children in any case; but my having given them the misfortune of such a father, endears them doubly to my heart: they are innocent—they depend upon me—and I feel this the most tender of all claims. While I live, my fondest attention shall be theirs!

All my life I loved the unfortunate, and ever will. Did you ever read Fielding's Amelia? If you have not, I beg you would. There are scenes in it, tender, domestic scenes, which I have read over and over, with feelings too delightful to describe! I meant a "Booth," as such a one infinitely to be preferred to a brutal, though perhaps constant husband. I can conceive a man fond of his wife, yet, (Sylvander-like,) hurried into a momentary deviation, while his heart remained faithful. If he concealed it, it could not hurt me; but if, unable to bear the anguish of self-reproach, he unbosomed it to me, I would not only forgive him, but comfort and speak kindly, and in secret only weep. Reconciliation, in such a case, would be exquisite beyond almost anything I can conceive! Do you now understand me on this subject? I was uneasy till it was explained; for all I have said, I know not if I had been an "Amelia," even with a "Booth." My resentments are keen, like all my other feelings: I am exquisitely alive to kindness and to unkindness. The first binds me for ever! But I have none of the spaniel in my nature. The last would soon cure me, though I loved to distraction. But all this is not, perhaps, interesting to Sylvander. I have seen nobody to-day; and, like a true egotist, talk away to please myself. I am not in a humour to answer your creed to-night.

I have been puzzling my brain about the fair one you bid me "not guess at."[10] I first thought it your Jean; but I don't know if she now possesses your "tenderest, faithfulest friendship." I can't understand that bonny lassie: her refusal, after such proofs of love, proves her to be either an angel or a dolt. I beg pardon; I know not all the circumstances, and am no judge therefore. I love you for your continued fondness, even after enjoyment: few of your sex have souls in such cases. But I take this to be the test of true love—mere desire is all the bulk of people are susceptible of; and that is soon satiated. "Your good wishes." You had mine, Sylvander, before I saw you. You will have them while I live. With you, I wish I had a little of the horse-cart in me. You and I have some horse properties; but more of the eagle, and too much of the turtle dove! Good night!

Your friend,
CLARINDA.

*Thursday Morning.*
This day is so good that I'll make out my call to your Square. I am laughing to myself at announcing this for the third time. Were she who "poisons your peace," to intend you a Pisgah view, she could do no more than I have done on this trivial occasion. Keep a good heart, Sylvander; the eternity of your love-sufferings will be ended before six weeks. Such perjuries the "Laughing gods allow." But remember, there is no such toleration in friendship, and

I am yours,
CLARINDA.

## LETTER XVII

SYLVANDER TO CLARINDA
[ *January 10th.* ]

I am certain I saw you, Clarinda; but you don't look to the proper story for a poet's lodging,

Where Speculation roosted near the sky.

I could almost have thrown myself over, for very vexation. Why didn't you look higher? It has spoilt my peace for this day. To be so near my charming Clarinda; to miss her look while it was searching for me. I am sure the soul is capable of disease; for mine has convulsed itself into an inflammatory fever. I am sorry for your little boy: do let me know to-morrow how he is.

You have converted me, Clarinda, (I shall love that name while I live: there is heavenly music in it.) Booth and Amelia I know well. Your sentiments on that subject, as they are on every subject, are just and noble. "To be feelingly alive to kindness and to unkindness," is a charming female character.

What I said in my last letter, the powers of fuddling sociality only know for me. By yours, I understand my good star has been partly in my horizon, when I got wild in my reveries. Had that evil planet, which has almost all my life shed its baleful rays on my devoted head, been as usual in its zenith, I had certainly blabbed something that would have pointed out to you the dear object of my tenderest friendship, and, in spite of me, something more. Had that fatal information escaped me, and it was merely chance or kind stars that it did not, I had been undone! You would never have written me, except, perhaps, *once* more! O, I could curse circumstances! and the coarse tie of human laws which keeps fast what common sense would loose, and which bars that happiness itself cannot give—happiness which otherwise love and honour would warrant! But hold—I shall make no more "hair-breadth 'scapes."

My friendship, Clarinda, is a life-rent business. My likings are both strong and eternal. I told you I had but one male friend: I have but two female. I should have a third, but she is surrounded by the blandishments of flattery and courtship. Her I register in my heart's core by Peggy Chalmers:* Miss Nimmo can tell you how divine she is. She is worthy of a place in the same bosom with my Clarinda. That is the highest compliment I can pay her. Farewell, Clarinda! Remember

SYLVANDER.
*Thursday, Noon.*

---

*Miss Margaret Chalmers was a highly-valued friend of Burns, with whom he corresponded, and upon whom he wrote one or two songs. In 1788 she married Mr Lewis Hay, a partner in the Banking-house of Sir William Forbes & Co. She resided many years at Pau, in Berne, where she died at an advanced age in the spring of 1843.

## LETTER XVIII

CLARINDA TO SYLVANDER

*Thursday Eve,* [ *January 10.* ]

I could not see you, Svlvander, though I had twice traversed the Square. I'm persuaded you saw not me neither. I met the young lady I meant to call for first; and returned to seek another acquaintance, but found her moved. All the time, my eye soared to poetic heights, *alias* garrets, but not a glimpse of you could I obtain You surely was within the glass, at least. I returned, finding my intrinsic dignity a good deal hurt, as I missed my friend. Perhaps I shall see you again next week: say how high you are. Thanks for your inquiry about my child; his complaints are of a tedious kind, and require patience and resignation. Religion has taught me both. By nature I inherit as little of them as a certain harum-scarum friend of mine. In what respects has Clarinda "converted you"? Tell me. It were an arduous task indeed!

Your "ravings" last night, and your ambiguous remarks upon them, I cannot, perhaps ought not to comprehend. I am your friend, Sylvander: take care lest virtue demand even friendship as a sacrifice. You need not curse the tie of human laws; since what is the happiness Clarinda would derive from being loosed? At present, she enjoys the hope of having her children provided for. In the other case, she is left, indeed, at liberty, but half dependent on the bounty of a friend,—kind in substantials, but having no feelings of romance: and who are the generous, the disinterested, who would risk the world's "dread laugh" to protect her and her little ones? Perhaps a Sylvander-like son of "whim and fancy" might, in a sudden fit of romance: but would not ruin be the consequence? Perhaps one of the former ★ ★ ★ yet if he was not dearer to her than all the world— such are still her romantic ideas—she could not be his.

You see, Sylvander, you have no cause to regret my bondage. The above is a true picture. Have I not reason to rejoice that I have it not in my power to dispose of myself? "I commit myself into thy hands, thou Supreme Disposer of all events! do with me as seemeth to thee good." Who is this one male friend? I know your third female. Ah, Sylvander! many "that are first shall be last," and *vice versa!* I am proud of being compared to Miss Chalmers:[11] I have heard how amiable she is. She cannot be more so than Miss Nimmo: why do ye not register her also? She is warmly your friend;—surely you are incapable of ingratitude. She has almost wept to me at mentioning your intimacy with a certain famous or infamous man in town. Do you think Clarinda could anger you just now? I composed lines addressed to you some time ago, containing a hint upon the occasion. I had not courage to send them then: if you say you'll not be angry, I will yet.

I know not how 'tis, but I felt an irresistible impulse to write you the moment I read yours. I have a design in it. Part of your interest in me is owing to mere novelty. You'll be tired of lily correspondence ere you leave town, and will never fash to write me from the country. I forgive you in a "state of celibacy." Sylvander, I wish I saw you happily married: you are so formed, you cannot be happy without a tender attachment. Heaven direct you!

When you see Bishop Geddes,★ ask him if he remembers a lady at Mrs Kemp's, on a Sunday night, who listened to every word he uttered with the gaze of attention. I saw he observed me, and returned that glance of cordial warmth which assured me he was pleased with my delicate flattery. I wished that night he had been my father, that I might shelter me in his bosom.

You shall have this, as you desired, to-morrow; and, if possible, none for four or five days. I say, if possible: for I really can't but write, as if I had nothing else to do. I admire your Epitaph; but while I read it, my heart swells at the sad idea of its realization. Did you ever read Sancho's Letters? they would hit your taste. My next will be on my favourite theme—religion.

Farewell, Sylvander! Be wise, be prudent, and be happy.
Clarinda.

Let your next be sent in the morning.

If you were well, I would ask you to meet me to-morrow, at twelve

---

★Bishop Geddes was the first clergyman of the Roman Catholic persuasion who had the degree of LL.D. conferred upon him after the Reformation. This took place in 1779; and redounds to the honour of the University of Aberdeen.

Soon afterwards, Bishop Geddes removed to London, and devoted himself to a new translation of the Scriptures, under the patronage of Lord Petre. Having, in the course of his studies, seen cause to change some of his views respecting scriptural authority and doctrine, he was viewed with distrust by those who considered themselves orthodox.

Bishop Geddes was a man of talents and learning, and published various works. He died in 1802.

o'clock. I go down in the Leith Fly, with poor Willie: what a Pleasant chat we might have! But I fancy 'tis impossible. Adieu!
*Friday, One o'clock.*

## LETTER XIX

SYLVANDER TO CLARINDA
*Saturday Morning, [ January 12.]*

Your thoughts on religion, Clarinda, shall be welcome. You may perhaps distrust me when I say 'tis also *my* favourite topic; but mine is the religion of the bosom. I hate the very idea of controversial divinity; as I firmly believe that every honest, upright man, of whatever sect, will be accepted of the Deity. If your verses, as you seem to hint, contain censure, except you want an occasion to break with me, don't send them. I have a little infirmity in my disposition, that where I fondly love or highly esteem I cannot bear reproach.

"Reverence thyself," is a sacred maxim; and I wish to cherish it. I think I told you Lord Bolingbroke's saying to Swift,—"Adieu, dear Swift! with all thy faults I love thee entirely: make an effort to love me with all mine." A glorious sentiment, and without which there can be no friendship! I do highly, very highly, esteem you indeed, Clarinda: you merit it all! Perhaps, too—I scorn dissimulation—I could fondly love you: judge, then, what a maddening sting your reproach would be. "Oh, I have sins to heaven, but none to you." With what pleasure would I meet you to-day, but I cannot walk to meet the Fly. I hope to be able to see you, *on foot,* about the middle of next week. I am interrupted—perhaps you are not sorry for it. You will tell me but I won't anticipate blame. O, Clarinda! did you know how dear to me is your look of kindness, your smile of approbation, you would not, either in prose or verse, risk a censorious remark.

> Curst be the verse, how well soe'er it flow,
> That tends to make one worthy man my foe.

SYLVANDER.★

---

★Between this and the ensuing letter there was probably one of Clarinda's, now lost.

## LETTER XX

~

SYLVANDER TO CLARINDA
[ *January 12.* ]

You talk of weeping, Clarinda: some involuntary drops wet your lines as I read them. Offend me, my dearest angel! You cannot offend me,—you never offended me. If you had ever given me the least shadow of offence, so pardon me my God as I forgive Clarinda. I have read yours again; it has blotted my paper. Though I find your letter has agitated me into a violent headache, I shall take a chair and be with you about eight. A friend is to be with us at tea, on my account, which hinders me from coming sooner. Forgive, my dearest Clarinda, my unguarded expressions! For Heaven's sake, forgive me, or I shall never be able to bear my own mind.

Your unhappy
SYLVANDER.

## LETTER XXI

~

CLARINDA TO SYLVANDER
*Sunday Evening,* [ *January 13.* ]

I will not deny it, Sylvander, last night was one of the most exquisite I ever experienced. Few such fall to the lot of mortals! Few, extremely few, are formed to relish such refined enjoyment. That it should be so, vindicates the wisdom of Heaven. But, though our enjoyment did not lead beyond the limits of virtue, yet today's reflections have not been altogether unmixed with regret. The idea of the pain it would have given, were it known to a friend to whom I am bound by the sacred ties of gratitude, (no more,) the opinion Sylvander may have formed from my unreservedness; and, above all, some secret misgivings that Heaven may not approve, situated as I am—these procured me a sleepless night; and, though at church, I am not at all well.

Sylvander, you saw Clarinda last night, behind the scenes! Now, you'll be convinced she has faults. If she knows herself, her intention is always good; but she is too often the victim of sensibility, and, hence, is seldom pleased with herself. A rencontre to-day I will relate to you, because it will show you I have my own share of pride. I

30

met with a sister of Lord Napier, at the house of a friend with whom I sat between sermons: I knew who she was; but paid her no other marks of respect than I do to any gentlewoman. She eyed me with minute, supercilious attention, never looking at me, when I spoke, but even half interrupted me, before I had done addressing the lady of the house. I felt my face glow with resentment, and consoled myself with the idea of being her superior in every respect but the accidental, trifling one of birth! I was disgusted at the fawning deference the lady showed her; and when she told me at the door that it was my Lord Napier's sister, I replied, "Is it, indeed? by her ill breeding I should have taken her for the daughter of some upstart tradesman!"

Sylvander, my sentiments as to birth and fortune are truly unfashionable: I despise the persons who pique themselves on either,—the former especially. Something may be allowed to bright talents, or even external beauty—these belong to us essentially; but birth in no respect can confer merit, because it is not our own. A person of a vulgar uncultivated mind I would not take to my bosom, in any station; but one possessed of natural genius, improved by education and diligence, such an one I'd take for my friend, be her extraction ever so mean. These, alone, constitute any real distinction between man and man. Are we not all the offspring of Adam? have we not one God? one Saviour? one Immortality? I have found but one among all my acquaintance who agreed with me—my Mary,* whom I mentioned to you. I am to spend to-morrow with her, if I am better. I like her the more that she likes you.

I intended to resume a little upon your favourite topic, the "Religion of the Bosom." Did you ever imagine that I meant any other? Poor were that religion and unprofitable whose seat was merely in the brain. In most points we seem to agree: only I found all my hopes of pardon and acceptance with Heaven upon the merit of Christ's atonement,—whereas you do upon a good life. You think "it helps weel, at least." If anything we could do had been able to atone for the violation of God's Law, where was the need (I speak it with reverence) of such an astonishing Sacrifice? Job was an "upright man."

*Miss Mary Peacock, afterwards the second wife of Mr James Gray of the High School of Edinburgh. They were both intimate friends of Mrs M'Lehose for many years.

Late in life Mr Gray went out to India, as a chaplain in the service of the East India Company. Honourable mention is made of them, in "Mrs Elwood's Overland Journey to India."

In the dark season of adversity, when other sins were brought to his remembrance, he boasted of his integrity; but no sooner did God reveal himself to him, than he exclaims: "Behold I am vile, and abhor myself in dust and ashes." Ah! my friend, 'tis pride that hinders us from embracing Jesus! we would be our own Saviour, and scorn to be indebted even to the "Son of the Most High." But this is the only sure foundation of our hopes. It is said by God Himself, "'tis to some a stumbling-block: to others foolishness;" but they who believe, feel it to be the "Wisdom of God, and the Power of God."

If my head did not ache, I would continue the subject. I, too, hate controversial religion; but this is the "Religion of the Bosom." My God! Sylvander, why am I so anxious to make you embrace the Gospel? I dare not probe too deep for an answer—let your heart answer: in a word—Benevolence. When I return, I'll finish this. Meantime, adieu! Sylvander, I intended doing you good: if it prove the reverse, I shall never forgive myself. Good night.

*Tuesday, Noon.*—Just returned front the Dean, where I dined and supped with fourteen of both sexes: all stupid. My Mary and I alone understood each other. However, we were joyous, and I sung in spite of my cold; but no wit. 'Twould have been pearls before swine literalized. I recollect promising to write you. Sylvander, you'll never find me worse than my word. If you have written me, (which I hope,) send it to me when convenient, either at nine in the morning or evening. I fear your limb may be worse from staying so late. I have other fears too: guess them! Oh my friend, I wish ardently to maintain your esteem; rather than forfeit one iota of it, I'd be content never to be wiser than now. Our last interview has raised you very high in mine. I have met with few, indeed, of your sex who understood delicacy in such circumstances; yet 'tis that only which gives a relish to such delightful intercourse. Do you wish to preserve my esteem, Sylvander? do not be proud to Clarinda! She deserves it not. I subscribe to Lord B.'s sentiment to Swift; yet some faults I shall still sigh over, though you style it reproach even to hint them. Adieu! You have it much in your power to add to the happiness or unhappiness of

CLARINDA.

## LETTER XXII

Sylvander to Clarinda.

*Monday Evening, 11 o'clock, [ Jan. 14th.]*

Why have I not heard from you, Clarinda? To-day I expected it; and, before supper, when a letter to me was announced, my heart danced with rapture; but behold, 'twas some fool who had taken into his head to turn poet, and made me an offering of the first fruits of his nonsense. It is not poetry, but "prose run mad."

Did I ever repeat to you an epigram I made on a Mr. Elphinstone,[12] who has given a translation of Martial, a famous Latin poet. The poetry of Elphinstone can only equal his prose notes. I was sitting in a merchant's shop of my acquaintance, waiting somebody; he put Elphinstone into my hand, and asked my opinion of it. I begged leave to write it on a blank leaf, which I did.

> To Mr Elphinstone, &c.
> O thou whom poesy abhors,
> Whom prose has turned out of doors,
> Heardst thou you groan? proceed no further,
> 'Twas laurel'd Martial calling murther.

I am determined to see you, if at all possible, on Saturday evening. Next week I must sing—

> The night is my departing night,
> The morn's the day I maun awa:
> There's neither friend nor foe of mine,
> But wishes that I were awa.
>
> What I hae done for lack o' wit,
> I never, never can reca';
> I hope ye're a' my friends as yet.
> Gude night, and joy be wi' you a'.[13]

If I could see you sooner, I would be so much the happier; but I would not purchase the dearest gratification on earth, if it must be at your expense in worldly censure, far less inward peace.

I shall certainly be ashamed of thus scrawling whole sheets of incoherence. The only unity (a sad word with poets and critics) in my ideas, is Clarinda.—There my heart "reigns and revels."

> What art thou, Love? whence are those charms,
> That thus thou bear'st an universal rule?

For thee the soldier quits his arms,
The king turns slave, the wise man fool.
In vain we chase thee from the field,
And with cool thoughts resist thy yoke;
Next tide of blood, alas! we yield,
And all those high resolves are broke!

I like to have quotations ready for every occasion. They give one's ideas so pat, and save one the trouble of finding expression adequate to one feelings. I think it is one of the greatest pleasures attending a poetic genius, that we can give our woes, cares, joys, loves, &c., an embodied form in verse, which, to me, is ever immediate ease. Goldsmith says finely of his muse—

Thou source of all my bliss and all my woe;
Who found'st me poor at first, and keep'st me so.

My limb has been so well to-day, that I have gone up and down stairs often without my staff. To-morrow I hope to walk once again on my own legs to dinner. It is only next street. Adieu!

SYLVANDER.

## LETTER XXIII

SYLVANDER TO CLARINDA
*Tuesday Evening,* [ *January 15.* ]

That you have faults, my Clarinda, I never doubted; but I knew not where they existed; and Saturday night made me more in the dark than ever. O, Clarinda! why would you wound my soul, by hinting that last night must have lessened my opinion of you. True, I was behind the scenes with you; but what did I see? A bosom glowing with honour and benevolence; a mind ennobled by genius, informed and refined by education and reflection, and exalted by native religion, genuine as in the climes of Heaven; a heart formed for all the glorious meltings of friendship, love, and pity. These I saw. I saw the noblest immortal soul creation ever showed me.

I looked long, my dear Clarinda, for your letter; and am vexed that you are complaining. I have not caught you so far wrong as in your idea—that the commerce you have with one friend hurts you, if you cannot tell every tittle of it to another. Why have so injurious a suspicion of a good God, Clarinda, as to think that Friendship and Love, on the sacred, inviolate principles of Truth, Honour and Religion, can be anything else than an object of His divine approbation? I have mentioned, in some of my former scrawls, Saturday evening next. Do allow me to wait on you that evening. Oh, my angel! how soon must we part!—and when can we meet again? I look forward on the horrid interval with tearful eyes. What have not I lost by not knowing you sooner!

I fear, I fear, my acquaintance with you is too short to make that lasting impression on your heart I could wish.

SYLVANDER

## LETTER XXIV

CLARINDA TO SYLVANDER
*Wednesday Morning,* [ *January 16th.*]

Your mother's wish was fully realized. I slept sounder last night than for weeks past—and I had a "blithe wakening": for your letter was the first object my eyes opened on. Sylvander, I fancy you and Vulcan are intimates: he has lent you a key which opens Clarinda's heart at pleasure, shows you what is there, and enables you to adapt yourself to its every feeling! I believe I shall give over writing you. Your letters are too much! my way is, alas! "hedged in"; but had I, like Sylvander, "the world before me," I should bid him, if he had a friend that loved me, tell him to write as he does, and "that would woo me." Seriously, you are the first letter-writer I ever knew. I only wonder how you can be fashed with my scrawls. I impute it to partialities. Either to-morrow or Friday I shall be happy to see you. On Saturday, I am not sure of being alone, or at home. Say which you'll come? Come to tea if you please; but eight will be an hour less liable to intrusions. I hope you'll *come afoot*, even though you take a chair home. A chair is so uncommon a thing in our neighbourhood, it is apt to raise speculation—but they are all asleep by ten. I am happy to hear of your being able to walk—even to the next street. You are a consummate flatterer; really my cheeks glow while I read your flights of Fancy. I fancy you see I like it, when you peep into the Repository. I know none insensible to that "delightful essence." If I grow affected or conceited, you are alone to blame. Ah, my friend! these are disgusting qualities! but I am not afraid. I know any merit I have perfectly—but I know many sad counterbalances.

Your lines on Elphinstone were clever, beyond anything I ever saw of the kind; I know the character—the figure is enough to make one cry, Murder! He is a complete pedant in language; but are not you and I pedants in something else? Yes, but in far superior things: Love, Friendship, Poesy, Religion! Ah, Sylvander! you have murdered Humility, and I can say thou didst it. You carry your warmth too far as to Miss Napier, (not Nairn;) yet I am pleased at it. She is sensible, lively, and well-liked they say. She was not to know Clarinda was "divine," and therefore kept her distance. She is comely, but a thick bad figure,—waddles in her pace, and has rosy cheeks.

I hate myself for being satirical—hate me for it too. I'll certainly go to Miers to please you, either with Mary or Miss Nimmo. Sylvander, some most interesting parts of yours I cannot enter on at present. I dare not think upon parting—upon the interval; but I am sure both are wisely ordered for our good. A line in return to tell me which night you'll be with me. "Lasting impression!" Your key might have shown you me better. Say, my lover, poet, and my friend, what day next month time Eternity will end? When you use your key, don't rummage too much, lost you find I am half as great a fool in the *tender* as yourself. Farewell! Sylvander. I may sign, for I am already sealed your friend,

Clarinda.

## LETTER XXV

Sylvander to Clarinda
*Sunday Night,* [ *January 20th.* ]

The impertinence of fools has joined with a return of an old indisposition to make me good for nothing to-day. The paper has lain before me all this evening to write to my dear Clarinda; but

Fools rush'd on fools, as waves succeed to waves.

I cursed them in my soul: they sacrilegiously disturb my meditations on her who holds my heart. What a creature is man! A little alarm last night, and to-day that I am mortal, has made such a revolution in my spirits! There is no philosophy, no divinity, comes half so home to the mind. I have no idea of courage that braves Heaven. 'Tis the wild ravings of an imaginary hero in Bedlam. I can no more, Clarinda; I can scarce hold up my head; but I am happy you don't know it, you would be so uneasy.

SYLVANDER

*Monday Morning.*

I am, my lovely friend, much better this morning, on the whole; but I have a horrid languor on my spirits.

> Sick of the world and all its joy,
> My soul in pining sadness mourns;
> Dark scenes of woe my mind employ,
> The past and present in their turns.

Have you ever met with a saying of the great and likewise good Mr Locke, author of the famous Essay on the Human Understanding? He wrote a letter to a friend, directing it "Not to be delivered till after my decease." It ended thus,—"I know you loved me when living, and will preserve my memory now I am dead. All the use to be made of it is, that this life affords no solid satisfaction, but in the consciousness of having done well, and the hopes of another life. Adieu! I leave my best wishes with you.—J. LOCKE."

Clarinda, may I reckon on your friendship for life? I think I may. Thou Almighty Preserver of men! Thy friendship, which hitherto I have too much neglected, to secure it shall, all the future days and nights of my life, be my steady care.

The idea of my Clarinda follows:—

> Hide it, my heart, within that close disguise,
> Where, mix'd with God's, her loved idea lies.[14]

But I fear inconstancy, the consequent imperfection of human weakness. Shall I meet with a friendship that defies years of absence and the chances and changes of fortune? Perhaps "such things are." *One* honest man I have great hopes from that way; but who, except a romance writer, would think on a *love* that could promise for life, in spite of distance, absence, chance, and change, and that, too, with slender hopes of fruition?

For my own part, I can say to myself in both requisitions—"Thou art the man." I dare, in cool resolve, I dare declare myself that friend and that lover. If womankind is capable of such things, Clarinda is. I trust that she is; and feel I shall be miserable if she is not. There is not one virtue which gives worth, or one sentiment which does honour to the sex, that she does not possess superior to any woman I ever saw: her exalted mind, aided a little, perhaps, by her situation, is, I think, capable of that nobly-romantic love-enthusiasm. May I see you on Wednesday evening, my dear angel? The next Wednesday again, will, I conjecture, be a hated day to us both. I tremble for censorious remarks, for your sake; but in extraordinary cases, may not usual and useful precaution be a little dispensed with? Three evenings, three swift-winged evenings, with pinions of down, are all the past—I dare not calculate the future. I shall call at Miss Nimmo tomorrow evening; 'twill be a farewell call.

I have written out my last sheet of paper, so I am reduced to my last half sheet. What a strange, mysterious faculty is that thing called imagination! We have no ideas almost at all, of another world; but I have often amused myself with visionary schemes of what happiness might be enjoyed by small alterations, alterations that we can fully enter to in this present state of existence. For instance: suppose you and I just as we are at present; the same reasoning powers, sentiments, and even desires; the same fond curiosity for knowledge and remarking observation in our minds; and imagine our bodies free from pain, and the necessary supplies for the wants of nature at all times and easily within our reach. Imagine, further, that we were set free from the laws of gravitation, which bind us to this globe, and could at pleasure fly, without inconvenience, through all the yet unconjectured bounds of creation; what a life of bliss should we lead in our mutual pursuit of virtue and knowledge, and our mutual enjoyment of friendship and love!

I see you laughing at my fairy fancies, and calling me a voluptuous Mahometan; but I am certain I should be a happy creature, beyond anything we call bliss here below: nay, it would be a paradise congenial to you too. Don't you see us hand in hand, or rather my arm about your lovely waist, making our remarks on Sirius, the nearest of the fixed stars; or surveying a comet flaming innoxious by us, as we just now would mark the passing pomp of a travelling monarch; or, in a shady bower of Mercury or Venus, dedicating the hour to love, in mutual converse, relying honour, and revelling endearment, while the most exalted strains of poesy and harmony would be the ready, spontaneous language of our souls! Devotion is the favourite employment of your heart; so is it of mine: what incentives then to, and powers for reverence, gratitude, faith, and hope, in all the fervour of adoration and praise to that Being, whose unsearchable wisdom, power, and goodness, so pervaded so inspired, every sense and feeling! By this time, I daresay, you will be blessing the neglect of the maid that leaves me destitute of paper.      SYLVANDER.

## LETTER XXVI

SYLVANDER TO CLARINDA
*Thursday Morning,* [ *Jan. 24.*]

Unlavish Wisdom never works in vain.

I have been tasking my reason, Clarinda, why a woman, who, for native genius, poignant wit, strength of mind, generous sincerity of soul, and the sweetest female tenderness, is without a peer; and whose personal charms have few, very few parallels among her sex; why, or how, she should fall to the blessed lot of a poor harum-scarum poet, whom Fortune had kept for her particular use to wreak her temper on, whenever she was in ill-humour.

One time I conjectured that, as Fortune is the most capricious jade ever known, she may have taken, not a fit of remorse, but a paroxysm of whim, to raise the poor devil out of the mire where he had so often, and so conveniently, served her as a stepping-stone, and given him the most glorious boon she ever had in her gift, merely for the maggot's sake, to see how his fool head and his fool heart will bear it.

At other times, I was vain enough to think that Nature, who has a great deal to say with Fortune, had given the coquettish goddess some such hint as—"Here is a paragon of female excellence, whose equal, in all my former compositions, I never was lucky enough to hit on, and despair of ever doing so again: you have cast her rather in the shades of life. There is a certain poet of my making: among your frolics, it would not be amiss to attach him to this masterpiece of my hand, to give her that immortality among mankind, which no woman of any age ever more deserved, and which few rhymesters of this age are better able to confer."

*Evening, Nine o'clock.*
I am here—absolutely unfit to finish my letter—pretty hearty, after a bowl which has been constantly plied since dinner till this moment. I have been with Mr Schetki the musician, and he has set the song★ finely. I have no distinct ideas of anything, but that I have drunk your health twice to-night, and that you are all my soul holds dear in this world.
SYLVANDER.

## LETTER XXVII

CLARINDA TO SYLVANDER
*Thursday Forenoon, [ January 24th. ]*

Sylvander, the moment I waked this morning, I received a summons from Conscience to appear at the Bar of Reason. While I trembled before this sacred throne, I beheld a succession of figures pass before me in awful brightness! Religion, clad in a robe of light, stalked majestically along, her hair dishevelled, and in her hand the Scriptures of Truth, held open at these words—"If you love me, keep my commandments." Reputation followed: her eyes darted indignation while she waved a beautiful wreath of laurel, intermixed with flowers, gathered by Modesty in the Bower of Peace. Consideration

★TO CLARINDA
Clarinda, mistress of my soul,
The measured time is run
The wretch beneath the dreary pole
So marks his latest sun.

To what dark cave of frozen night
Shall poor Sylvander hie,
Deprived of thee, his life and light—
The sun of all his joy?

We part—but by those precious drops,
That fill thy lovely eyes
No other light shall guide my steps,
Till thy bright beams arise.

She, the fair sun of all her sex,
Uas blest my glorious day;
And shall a glimmering planet fix
My worship to its ray?

held her bright mirror close to my eyes, and made me start at my own image! Love alone appeared as counsel in my behalf. She was adorned with a veil, borrowed from Friendship, which hid her defects, and set off her beauties to advantage. She had no plea to offer, but that of being the sister of Friendship, and the offspring of Charity. But Reason refused to listen to her defence, because she brought no certificate from the Temple of Hymen! While I trembled before her, Reason addressed me in the following manner:—"Return to my paths, which alone are peace; shut your heart against the fascinating intrusion of the passions; take Consideration for your guide, and you will soon arrive at the Bower of Tranquillity."

Sylvander, to drop my metaphor, I am neither well nor happy to-day: my heart reproaches me for last night. If you wish Clarinda to regain her peace, determine against everything but what the strictest delicacy warrants.

I do not blame you, but myself. I must not see you on Saturday, unless I find I can depend on myself acting otherwise. Delicacy, you know, it was which won me to you at once: take care you do not loosen the dearest, most sacred tie that unites us? Remember Clarinda's present and eternal happiness depends upon her adherence to Virtue. Happy Sylvander! that can be attached to Heaven and Clarinda together. Alas! I feel I cannot serve two masters. God pity me!

*Thursday Night.*
Why have I not heard from you, Sylvander? Everything in nature seems tinged with gloom to-day. Ah! Sylvander—

> The heart's ay the part ay
> That makes us right or wrang!

How forcibly have these lines recurred to my thoughts! Did I not tell you what a wretch love rendered me? Affection to the strongest height, I am capable of, to a man of my Sylvander's merit—if it did not lead me into weaknesses and follies my heart utterly condemns. I am convinced, without the approbation of Heaven and my own mind, existence would be to me a heavy curse. Sylvander, why do not your Clarinda's repeated levities cure the too passionate fondness you express for her? Perhaps it has a little removed esteem. But I dare not touch this string—it would fill up the cup of my present misery. Oh, Sylvander, may the friendship of that God, you and I have too much neglected to secure, be henceforth our chief study and delight. I cannot live deprived of the consciousness of His favour. I feel something of this awful state all this day. Nay, while I approached God with my lips, my heart was not fully there.

Mr Locke's posthumous letter ought to be written in letters of gold.—What heartfelt joy does the consciousness of having done well in any one instance confer; and what agony the reverse! Do not be displeased when I tell you I wish our parting was over. At a distance we shall retain the same heartfelt affection and interestedness in each other's concerns;—but absence will mellow and restrain those violent heart-agitations which, if continued much longer, would unhinge my very soul, and render me unfit for the duties of life. You and I are capable of that ardency of love, for which the wide creation cannot afford an adequate object. Let us seek to repose it in the bosom of our God. Let us next give a place to those dearest on earth—the tender charities of parent, sister, child! I bid you good night with this short prayer of Thomson's—

> Father of Light and Life, thou good Supreme!
> Oh teach us what is good—teach us Thyself!
> Save us from Folly, Vanity, and Vice, &c.

Your letter—I should have liked had it contained a little of the last one's seriousness. Bless me!—You must not flatter so; but it's in a "merry mood," and I make allowances. Part of some of your encomiums, I know I deserve; but you are far out when you enumerate "strength of mind" among them. I have not even an ordinary share of it—every passion does what it will with me; and all my life, I have been guided by the impulse of the moment—unsteady, and weak! I thank you for the letter, though it sticket my prayer. Why did you tell me you drank away Reason, "that Heaven-lighted lamp in man"? When Sylvander utters a calm, sober sentiment, he is never half so charming. I have read several of these in your last letter with vast pleasure. Good night!

*Friday Morning.*
My servant[15] (who is a good soul) will deliver you this. She is going down to Leith, and will return about two or three o'clock. I have ordered her to call then, in case you have ought to say to Clarinda to-day. I am better of that sickness at my heart I had yesterday; but

there's a sting remains, which will not be removed till. I am at peace with Heaven and myself. Another interview, spent as we ought, will help to procure this. A day when the sun shines gloriously, always makes me devout! I hope 'tis an earnest (to-day) of being soon restored to the "light of His countenance," who is the source of love and standard of perfection. Adieu!

CLARINDA.

## LETTER XXVIII

SYLVANDER TO CLARINDA
[ *January 25.* ]

Clarinda, my life, you have wounded my soul. Can I think of your being unhappy, even though it be not described in your pathetic elegance of language, without being miserable? Clarinda, can I bear to be told from you that "you will not see me to-morrow night—that you wish the hour of parting were come!" Do not let us impose on ourselves by sounds. If, in the moment of fond endearment and tender dalliance, I perhaps trespassed against the *letter* of Decorum's law, I appeal, even to you, whether I ever sinned, in the very least degree, against the *spirit* of her strictest statute? But why, my love, talk to me in such strong terms; every word of which cuts me to the very soul? You know a hint, the slightest signification of your wish, is to me a sacred command.

Be reconciled, my angel, to your God, yourself, and me; and I pledge you Sylvander's honour—an oath, I daresay, you will trust without reserve, that you shall never more have reason to complain of his conduct. Now, my love, do not wound our next meeting with any averted looks or restrained caresses. I have marked the line of conduct—a line, I know, exactly to your taste—and which I will inviolably keep; but do not you show the least inclination to make boundaries. Seeming distrust, where you know you may confide, is a cruel sin against sensibility.

"Delicacy, you know, it was which won me to you at once: take care you do not loosen the dearest, most sacred tie that unites us." Clarinda, I would not have stung *your* soul—I would not have bruised *your* spirit, as that harsh crucifying "Take care" did *mine*; no, not to have gained heaven! Let me again appeal to your dear self, if Sylvander, even when he seemingly half transgressed the laws of decorum, if he did not show more chastised, trembling, faltering delicacy, than the many of the world do in keeping these laws?

Oh Love and Sensibility, ye have conspired against my Peace! I love to madness, and I feel to torture! Clarinda, how can I forgive myself, that I have ever touched a single chord in your bosom with pain! would I do it willingly? Would any consideration, any gratification, make me do so? Oh, did you love like me, you would not, you could not, deny or put off a meeting with the man who adores you;—who would die a thousand deaths before he would injure you; and who must soon bid you a long farewell!

I had proposed bringing my bosom friend, Mr Ainslie,[16] to-morrow evening, at his strong request, to see you; as he has only time to stay with us about ten minutes, for an engagement. But I shall hear from you: this afternoon, for mercy's sake!—for, till I hear from you, I am wretched.

O Clarinda, the tie that binds me to thee is in-twisted, incorporated with my dearest threads of life!

SYLVANDER.

## LETTER XXIX

SYLVANDER TO CLARINDA
[ *January 26th.* ]

I was on the way, my *Love,* to meet you, (I never do things by halves,) when I got your card. Mr Ainslie goes out of town to-morrow morning, to see a brother of his who is newly arrived from France. I am determined that he and I shall call on you together. So, look you, lest I should never see to-morrow, we will call on you to-night. Mary and you may put off tea till about seven, at which time, in the Galloway phrase, "an' the beast be to the fore, and the branks bide hale," expect the humblest of your humble servants, and his dearest friend. We only propose staying half an hour—"for ought we ken." I could suffer the lash of misery eleven months in the year, were the twelfth to be composed of hours like yesternight. You are the soul of my enjoyment; all else is of the stuff of stocks and stones.

SYLVANDER.

## LETTER XXX

SYLVANDER TO CLARINDA
*Sunday, Noon,* [ *Jan. 27th.* ]

I have almost given up the Excise idea. I have been just now to wait on a great person, Miss ———'s friend, ———.[17] Why will great people not only deafen us with the din of their equipage, and dazzle us with their fastidious pomp, but they must also be so very dictatorially wise? I have been questioned like a child about my matters, and blamed and schooled for my Inscription on Stirling window.[18] Come, Clarinda!—"Come, curse me, Jacob; come, defy me, Israel!"

*Sunday Night.*

I have been with Miss Nimmo. She is, indeed, "a good soul," as my Clarinda finely says. She has reconciled me, in a good measure, to the world with her friendly prattle.

   Schetki has sent me the song, set to a fine air of his composing. I have called the song Clarinda:★ I have carried it about in my pocket and thumbed it over all day.

*Monday Morning.*

If my prayers have any weight in heaven, this morning looks in on you and finds you in the arms of peace, except where it is charmingly interrupted by the ardours of devotion. I find so much serenity of mind, so much positive pleasure, so much fearless daring toward the world, when I warm in devotion, or feel the glorious sensation— a consciousness of Almighty friendship—that I am sure I shall soon be an honest enthusiast.

> How are thy servants blest, O Lord!
> How sure is their defence!
> Eternal wisdom is their guide,
> Their help Omnipotence.

I am, my dear Madam, yours,
SYLVANDER.

★ See page [40].

## LETTER XXXI

CLARINDA TO SYLVANDER

*Sunday, Eight Evening,* [*27th.*]

Sylvander, when I think of you as my dearest and most attached friend, I am highly pleased; but when you come across my mind as my lover, something within gives a sting resembling that of guilt. Tell me why is this? It must be from the idea that I am another's. What! another's wife. Oh cruel Fate! I am, indeed, bound in an iron chain. Forgive me, if this should give you pain. You know I must (I told you I must) tell you my genuine feelings, or be silent. Last night we were happy beyond what the bulk of mankind can conceive. Perhaps the "line" you had marked was a little infringed,—it was really; but, though I disapprove, I have not been unhappy about it. I am convinced no less of your discernment, than of your wish to make your Clarinda happy. I know you sincere, when you profess horror at the idea of what would render her miserable for ever. Yet we must guard against going to the verge of danger. Ah! my friend, much need had we to "watch and pray!" May those benevolent spirits, whose office it is to save the fall of Virtue struggling on the brink of Vice, be ever present to protect and guide us in right paths!

I had an hour's conversation to-day with my worthy friend Mr Kemp.★[19] You'll attribute, perhaps, to this, the above sentiments. 'Tis true, there's not one on earth has so much influence on me, except— Sylvander; partly it has forced me "to feel along the Mental Intelligence." However, I've broke the ice. I confessed I had conceived a tender impression of late—that it was mutual, and that I had wished to unbosom myself to him, (as I always did,) particularly to ask if he thought I should, or not, mention it to my friend? I saw he felt for me, (for I was in tears;) but he bewailed that I had given my heart while in my present state of bondage; wished I had made it friendship only; in short, talked to me in the style of a tender parent, anxious for my happiness. He disapproves altogether of my saying a syllable of the matter to my friend,—says it could only make him uneasy; and that I am in no way bound to do it by any one tie. This has eased

★The Reverend John Kemp, minister of the Tolbooth Church, Edinburgh; a man of acknowledged acquirements and ability, and of high standing in society. He twice intermarried with the nobility.

me of a load which has lain upon my mind ever since our intimacy.
Sylvander, I wish you and Mr Kemp were acquainted,—such worth
and sensibility! If you had his piety and sobriety of manners, united
to the shining abilities you possess, you'd be "a faultless monster
which the world ne'er saw." He, too, has great talents. His imagination is rich—his feelings delicate—his discernment acute; yet there
are shades in his, as in all characters: but these it would ill become
Clarinda to point out. Alas! I know too many blots in my own.

Sylvander, I believe nothing were a more impracticable task than
to make you feel a little of genuine gospel humility. Believe me, I
wish not to see you deprived of that noble fire of an exalted mind
which you eminently possess. Yet a sense of your faults—a feeling
sense of them!—were devoutly to be wished. Tell me, did you ever,
or how oft have you smote on your breast, and cried, "God be merciful to me a sinner"? I fancy, once or twice, when suffering from the
effects of your errors. Pardon me if I be hurting your "intrinsic dignity; it need not—even "divine Clarinda" has been in this mortal
predicament.

Pray, what does Mr Ainslie think of her? Was he not astonished to
find her merely human? Three weeks ago, I suppose you would have
made him walk into her presence unshod: but one must bury even
divinities when they discover symptoms of mortality!—(Let these
be interred in Sylvander's bosom.)

My dearest friend, there are two wishes uppermost in my heart:
to see you think alike with Clarinda on religion, and settled in some
creditable line of business. The warm interest I take in both these, is,
perhaps, the best proof of the sincerity of my friendship—as well as
earnest of its duration. As to the first, I devolve it over into the hands
of the Omniscient! May he raise up friends who will effectuate the
other While I breathe these fervent wishes, think not anything but
pure disinterested regard prompts them. They are fond but chimerical
ideas. They are never indulged but in the hour of tender endearment,
when

> —Innocence
> Looked gaily smiling on, while rosy Pleasure
> Hid young Desire amid her flowery wreath,
> And poured her cup luxuriant, mantling high
> The sparkling, Heavenly vintage—Love and Bliss.

'Tis past ten—and I please myself with thinking Sylvander will be about to retire, and write to Clarinda. I fancy you'll find this stupid enough; but I can't be always bright—the sun will be sometimes under a cloud. Sylvander, I wish our kind feelings were more moderate; why set one's heart upon impossibilities? Try me merely as your friend (alas, all I ought to be.)

Believe me, you'll find me most rational. If you'd caress the "mental intelligence" as you do the corporeal frame, indeed, Sylvander you'd make me a philosopher. I see you fidgeting at this violently, blasting rationality. I have a headache which brings home these things to the mind. To-morrow I'll hear from you, I hope. This is Sunday, and not a word on our favourite subject. O fy, "divine Clarinda." I intend giving you my idea of Heaven in opposition to your heathenish description, (which, by the by, was elegantly drawn.) Mine shall be founded on Reason and supported by Scripture; but it's too late, my head aches, but my heart is affectionately yours.

*Monday Morning.*

I am almost not sorry at the Excise affair misgiving. You will be better out of Edinburgh—it is full of temptation to one of your social turn.

Providence (if you be wise in future) will order something better for you. I am half glad you were schooled about the Inscription; 'twill be a lesson, I hope, in future. Clarinda would have lectured you on it before, "if she dared." Miss Nimmo is a woman after my own heart. You are reconciled to the world by her "friendly prattle"! How can you talk so diminutively of the conversation of a woman of solid sense? what will you say of Clarinda's chit chat? I suppose you would give it a still more insignificant term if you dared; but it is mixed with something that makes it bearable, were it even weaker than it is. Miss Nimmo is right in both her conjectures. Ah, Sylvander! my peace must suffer—yours cannot. You think, in loving Clarinda, you are doing right: all Sylvander's eloquence cannot convince me that it is so! If I were but at liberty—Oh how I would indulge in all the luxury of innocent love! It is, I fear, too late to talk in this strain, after indulging you and myself so much; but would Sylvander shelter his Love in Friendship's allowed garb, Clarinda would be far happier.

To-morrow, didst thou say? The time is short now—is it not too frequent? do not sweetest dainties cloy soonest? Take your chance—come half-past eight. If anything particular occur to render it improper to-morrow, I'll send you word, and name another evening. Mr —— is to call to-night, I believe. He, too, trembles for my peace. Two such worthies to be interested about my foolish ladyship! The Apostle Paul, with all his rhetoric, could not reconcile me to the great (little souls) when I think of them and Sylvander together; but I pity them.

> If e'er ambition did my fancy cheat,
> With any wish so mean, as to be great,
> Continue, Heaven, far from me to remove
> The humble blessings of that life I love.

Till we meet, my dear Sylvander, adieu!
CLARINDA

## LETTER XXXII

SYLVANDER TO CLARINDA
*Sunday Morning,* [*27th January.*]

I have just been before the throne of my God, Clarinda. According to my association of ideas, my sentiments of love and friendship, I next devote myself to you. Yesternight I was happy—happiness "that the world cannot give." I kindle at the recollection; but it is a flame where Innocence looks smiling on, and Honour stands by, a sacred guard. Your heart, your fondest wishes, your dearest thoughts, these are yours to bestow: your person is unapproachable, by the laws of your country; and he loves not as I do who would make you miserable.

You are an angel Clarinda: you are surely no mortal that "the earth owns." To kiss your hand, to live on your smile, is to me far more exquisite bliss, than any the dearest favours that the fairest of the sex, yourself excepted, can bestow.

*Sunday Evening.*

You are the constant companion of my thoughts. How wretched is the condition of one who is haunted with conscious guilt, and trembling under the idea of dreaded vengeance! And what a placid calm, what a charming secret enjoyment is given to one's bosom by the kind feelings of friendship, and the fond throes of love! Out upon the tempest of Anger, the acrimonious gall of fretful Impatience, the sullen frost of lowering Resentment, or the corroding poison of withered Envy! They eat up the immortal part of man! If they spent their fury only on the unfortunate objects of them, it would be something in their favour; but these miserable passions, like traitor Iscariot, betray their Lord and Master.

Thou Almighty Author of peace and goodness, and love! do Thou give me the social heart that kindly tastes of every man's cup! Is it a draught of joy?—warm and open my heart to share it with cordial, unenvying rejoicing! Is it the bitter potion of sorrow?—melt my heart with sincerely sympathetic woe! Above all, do Thou give me the manly mind, that resolutely exemplifies in life and manners those sentiments which I would wish to be thought to possess! The friend of my soul— there may I never deviate from the firmest fidelity and most active kindness! Clarinda, the dear object of my fondest love; there, may the most sacred, inviolate honour, the most faithful, kindling constancy, ever watch and animate my every thought and imagination!

Did you ever meet the following lines spoken of Religion, your darling topic?—

> 'Tis *this*, my friend, that streaks our morning bright!
> 'Tis *this* that gilds the horror of our night!
> When wealth forsakes us, and when friends are few;
> When friends are faithless, or when foes pursue;
> 'Tis this that wards the blow or stills the smart,
> Disarms affliction, or repels its dart:
> Within the breast bids purest rapture rise,
> Bids smiling Conscience spread her cloudless skies.

I met with these verses very early in life, and was so delighted with them that I have them by me, copied at school.

Good night, and sound rest,

My dearest Clarinda.

SYLVANDER.

## LETTER XXXIII

CLARINDA TO SYLVANDER
*Wednesday Evening, Nine, [ Jan. 30]*

There is not a sentiment in your last dear letter but must meet the approbation of every worthy discerning mind—except one—"that my heart, my fondest wishes," are mine to bestow. True, they are not, they cannot be placed upon him who ought to have had them, but whose conduct, (I dare not say more against him,) has justly forfeited them. But is it not too near an infringement of the sacred obligations of marriage to bestow one's heart, wishes, and thoughts upon another? Something in my soul whispers that it approaches criminality. I obey the voice. Let me cast every kind feeling into the allowed bond of Friendship. If 'tis accompanied with a shadow of a softer feeling it shall be poured into the bosom of a merciful God! If a confession of my warmest, tenderest friendship does not satisfy you, duty forbids Clarinda should do more! Sylvander, I never expect to be happy here below! Why was I formed so susceptible of emotions I dare not indulge? Never were there two hearts formed so exactly alike, as ours! No wonder our friendship is heightened by the "sympathetic glow." In reading your Life, I find the very first poems that hit your fancy, were those that first engaged mine. While almost a child, the hymn you mentioned, and another of Addison's,"When all thy mercies," &c., were my chief favourites. They are much so to this hour; and I make my boys repeat them every Sabbath day. When about fifteen, I took a great fondness for Pope's "Messiah," which I still reckon one of the sublimest pieces I ever met with.

Sylvander, I believe our friendship will be lasting; its basis has been virtue, similarity of tastes, feelings, and sentiments. Alas! I shudder at the idea of an hundred miles distance. You'll hardly write me once a-month, and other objects will weaken your affection for Clarinda. Yet I cannot believe so. Oh, let the scenes of Nature remind you of Clarinda! In winter, remember the dark shades of her fate; in summer, the warmth, the cordial warmth, of her friendship; in autumn, her glowing wishes to bestow plenty on all; and let spring animate you with hopes, that your friend may yet live to surmount the wintry blasts of life, and revive to taste a spring-time of happiness! At all events, Sylvander, the storms of life will quickly pass, and "one unbounded spring encircle all." There, Sylvander, I trust we'll meet. Love, there, is not a crime. I charge you to meet me there—Oh, God!—I must lay down my pen.—I repent, almost, flattering your writing talents so much: I can see you know all the merit you possess. The allusion of the key is true—therefore I won't recant it; but I rather was too humble about my own letters. I have met with several who wrote worse than myself, and few, of my own sex, better; so I don't give you great credit for being fashed with them.

Sylvander, I have things with different friends I can't tell to another, yet am not hurt; but I told you of that particular friend:[20] he was, for near four years, the one I confided in. He is very worthy, and answers your description in the "Epistle to J. S." exactly. When I had hardly a friend to care for me in Edinburgh, he befriended me. I saw, too soon, 'twas with him a warmer feeling: perhaps a little infection was the natural effect. I told you the circumstances which helped to eradicate the tender impression in me; but I perceive (though he never tells me so)—I see it in every instance—*his* prepossession still remains. I esteem him as a faithful friend; but I can never feel more for him. I fear he's not convinced of that. He sees no man with me half so often as himself; and thinks I surely am at least partial to no other. I cannot bear to deceive one in so tender a point, and am hurt at his harbouring an attachment I never can return. I have thoughts of owning my intimacy with Sylvander; but a thousand things forbid it. I should be tortured with Jealousy, that "green-eyed monster;" and, besides, I fear 'twould wound his peace. 'Tis a delicate affair. I wish your judgment on it. O Sylvander, I cannot bear to give pain to any creature, far less to one who pays me the attention of a brother!

I never met with a man congenial, perfectly congenial to myself but *one*—ask no questions. Is Friday to be the last night? I wish, Sylvander, you'd steal away—I cannot bear farewell! I can hardly relish the idea of meeting—for the idea but we will meet again, at least in Heaven, I hope. Sylvander, when I survey myself, my returning weaknesses, I am consoled that my hopes, my immortal hopes, are founded in the complete righteousness of a compassionate Saviour. "In all our afflictions, He is afflicted, and the angel of His presence guards us."

I am charmed with the Lines on Religion, and with you for relishing them. I only wish the world saw you, as you appear in your letters to me. Why did you send forth to them the "Holy Fair," &c.? Had Clarinda known you, she would have held you in her arms till she had your promise to suppress them.[21] Do not publish the "Moor Hen." Do not, for your sake, and for mine. I wish you vastly to hear my valued friend, Mr Kemp. Come to hear him on Sunday afternoon. 'Tis the first favour I have asked you: I expect you'll not refuse me. You'll easily get a seat. Your favourite, Mr Gould, I admired much. His composition is elegant indeed!—but 'tis like beholding a beautiful superstructure built on a sandy foundation: 'tis fine to look upon; but one dares not abide in it with safety. Mr Kemp's language is very good,—perhaps not such studied periods as Mr G.'s; but he is far more animated. He is pathetic in a degree that touches one's soul! and then, 'tis all built upon a rock.

I could chide you for the Parting Song. It wrings my heart. "You may reca'"—by being wise in future—"your friend as yet." I will be your friend for ever! Good night! God bless you! prays

CLARINDA.

*Thursday, Noon.*
I shall go to-morrow forenoon to Miers★ alone: 'tis quite a usual thing I hear. Mary is not in town; and I don't care to ask Miss Nimmo, or anybody else. What size do you want it about? O Sylvander, if you wish my peace, let Friendship be the word between us: I tremble at more. "Talk not of Love," &c. To-morrow I'll expect you. Adieu!

CLARINDA.

---

## LETTER XXXIV

SYLVANDER TO CLARINDA
*Thursday Night, [ January 31]*

I cannot be easy, my Clarinda, while any sentiment respecting me in your bosom gives you pain. If there is no man on earth to whom your heart and affections are justly due, it may savour of imprudence, but never of criminality, to bestow that heart and those affections where you please. The God of love meant and made those delicious attachments to be bestowed on somebody; and even all the imprudence lies in bestowing them on an unworthy object. If this reasoning is conclusive, as it certainly is, I must be allowed to "talk of Love."

It is, perhaps, rather wrong to speak highly to a friend of his letter: it is apt to lay one under a little restraint in their future letters, and restraint is the death of a friendly epistle; but there is one passage in

---

★Miers was a miniature painter of that time. A profile of Burns by him appears in Hogg and Motherwell's edition of the Poet's Works.

your last charming letter, Thomson nor Shenstone never exceeded it, nor often came up to it. I shall certainly steal it, and set it in some future poetic production, and get immortal fame by it. 'Tis when you bid the scenes of nature remind me of Clarinda. Can I forget you, Clarinda? I would detest myself as a tasteless, unfeeling, insipid, infamous blockhead! I have loved women of ordinary merit, whom I could have loved for ever. You are the first, the only unexceptionable individual of the beauteous sex that I ever met with; and never woman more entirely possessed my soul. I know myself, and how far I can depend on passions, well. It has been my peculiar study.

I thank you for going to Miers. Urge him, for necessity calls, to have it done by the middle of next week: Wednesday the latest day. I want it for a breast-pin, to wear next my heart. I propose to keep sacred set times, to wander in the woods and wilds for meditation on you. Then, and only then, your lovely image shall be produced to the day, with a reverence akin to devotion.

★   ★   ★   ★   ★   ★   ★   ★   ★   ★   ★
★   ★   ★   ★   ★   ★   ★   ★   ★   ★   ★
★   ★   ★   ★   ★   ★   ★   ★   ★   ★   ★

To-morrow night shall not be the last. Good night! I am perfectly stupid, as I supped late yesternight.

SYLVANDER.

## LETTER XXXV

CLARINDA TO SYLVANDER

*Saturday Evening, [February 2d.]*

I am wishing, Sylvander, for the power of looking into your heart. It would be but fair—for you have the key of mine. You are possessed of acute discernment. I am not deficient either in that respect. Last night must have shown you Clarinda not "divine"—but as she really is. I cant recollect some things I said without a degree of pain. Nature has been kind to me in several respects; but one essential she has denied me entirely: it is that instantaneous perception of fit and unfit, which is so useful in the conduct of life. No one can discriminate more accurately afterwards than Clarinda. But when her heart is expanded by the influence of kindness, she loses all command of it, and often suffers severely in the recollection of her unguardedness.

You must have perceived this; but, at any rate, I wish you to know me, as "I really am." I would have given much for society to-day; for I can't bear my own: but no human being has come near me. Well as I like you, Sylvander, I would rather lose your love, than your esteem: the first I ought not to wish; the other I shall ever endeavour to maintain. But no more of this: you prohibit it, and I obey.

For many years, have I sought for a male friend, endowed with sentiments like yours; one who could love me with tenderness, yet unmixed with selfishness: who could be my friend, companion, protector, and who would die sooner than injure me. I sought—but I sought in vain! Heaven has, I hope, sent me this blessing in my Sylvander! Whatever weaknesses may cleave to Clarinda, her heart is not to blame: whatever it may have been by nature, it is unsullied by art. If she dare dispose of it—last night can leave you at no loss to guess the man:

> Then, dear Sylvander, use it weel,
> An' row it in your bosom's biel;
> Ye'll find it aye baith kind and leal,
>     And fou o' glee;
> It wad nae wrang the vera deil,—
>     Ah, far less thee![22]

How do you like this parody on a passage of my favourite poet?—it is extempore—from the heart; and let it be to the heart. I am to enclose the first fruits of my muse, "To a Blackbird."* It has no poetic merit; but it bespeaks a sweet feminine mind—such a one as I wish mine to be; but my vivacity deprives me of that softness which is, in my opinion, the first female ornament. It was written to soothe an aching heart. I then laboured under a cruel anguish of soul, which I cannot tell you of. If I ever take a walk to the Temple of H——, I'll disclose it; but you and I (were it even possible) would "fall out by the way." The lines on the Soldier were occasioned by reading a book entitled the "Sorrows of the Heart." Miss Nimmo was pleased with them, and sent them to the gentleman. They are not poetry, but they speak what I felt at a survey of so much filial tenderness.

I agree with you in liking quotations. If they are apt, they often give one's ideas more pleasantly than our own language can at all times. I am stupid to-night. I have a soreness at my heart. I conclude,

*See Appendix.

therefore, with a verse of Goldsmith, which, of late, has become an immense favourite of mine:—

> In Nature's simplest habit clad,
>     No wealth nor power had he;
> Genius and worth were all he had,
>     But these were all to me.

Good night, "my dear Sylvander;" say this (like Werter) to yourself.
Your CLARINDA.

*Sunday Evening.*

I would have given much, Sylvander, that you had heard Mr Kemp this afternoon. You would have heard my principles, and the foundation of all my immortal hopes, elegantly delivered. "Let me live the life of the righteous, and my latter end be like his," was the text. Who are the righteous? "Those," says Sylvander, "whose minds are actuated and governed by purity, truth, and charity." But where does such a mind exist? It must be where the "soul is made perfect," for I know none such on earth. "The righteous," then, must mean those who believe in Christ, and rely on his perfect righteousness for their salvation. "Everlasting" life, as you observe, it is in the power of all to embrace; and this is eternal life, to "believe in Him whom God hath sent." Purity, truth, and charity will flow from this belief, as naturally as the stream from the fountain. These are, indeed, the only evidences we can have of the reality of our faith; and they must be produced in a degree ere we can be fit for the enjoyment of Heaven. But where is the man who dare plead these before "Infinite Holiness"? Will Inflexible Justice pardon our thousand violations of his laws? Will our imperfect repentance and amendments atone for past guilt? or, will we presume to present our best services (spotted as they are) as worthy of acceptance before Unerring Rectitude? I am astonished how any intelligent mind, blessed with a divine revelation, can pause a moment on the subject. "Enter not into judgment with me, O Lord! In thy sight no flesh can be justified!" This must be the result of every candid mind, upon surveying its own deserts. if God had not been pleased to reveal His own Son, as our all-sufficient Saviour, what could we have done but cried for mercy, without sure hope of obtaining it? But when we have Him clearly announced as our surety, our guide, our blessed advocate with the Father, who, in their senses, ought to hesitate, in putting their souls into the hands of this glorious "Prince of Peace"? Without this, we may admire the Creator in his works, but we can never approach him with the confidential tenderness of children. "I will arise, and go to my father." This is the blessed language of every one who believes and trusts in Jesus. Oh, Sylvander, who would go on fighting with themselves, resolving and re-resolving, while they can thus fly to their Father's house? But, alas! it is not till we tire of these husks of our own, that we recollect that *there*, there is bread enough, and to spare. Whenever the wish is sincerely formed in our hearts, our Heavenly Father will have compassion upon us—"though a great way off." This is the "religion of the bosom." I BELIEVE that there will be many of every sect, nation, and people, who will "stand before the throne"; but I believe that it will be the effect of Christ's atonement, conveyed to them by ways too complicated for our finite minds to comprehend. But why should we, who know "the way, the truth, and the life," deprive ourselves of the comfort it is fitted to yield? Let my earnest wish for your eternal, as well as temporal happiness, excuse the warmth with which I have unfolded what has been my own fixed point of rest. I want no controversy—I hate it; let our only strivings be, who shall be the most constant and attached friend,—which of us shall render our conduct most approved to the other. I am well aware how vain it were (vain in every sense of the expression) to hope to sway a mind so intelligent as yours, by any arguments I could devise. May that God, who spoke worlds into existence, open your eyes to see "the truth, as it is in Jesus!" Forgive me, Sylvander, if I've been tedious upon my favourite theme. You know who it was, who could not stop when his divinity came across him. Even there you see we are congenial.

I'll tell you a pretty apt quotation I made to-day, warm from my heart. I met the Judges in the morning, as I went into the Parliament Square, among whom was Lord Dreghorn,* in his new robes of purple. He is my mother's cousin-german, the greatest real honour he could ever claim; but used me in a manner unfeeling, harsh beyond

*Lord Dreghorn was the son of Colin Maclaurin, the celebrated mathematician, and after a successful practice at the bar, was raised to the Bench. He published several works, and died in 1796. Many of the Judges, at that period, went in their robes to the High Church, in Parliament Square.

description, at one of the darkest periods of my chequered life. I looked steadfastly in his sour face; his eye met mine. I was a female, and therefore he stared; but, when he knew who it was, he averted his eyes suddenly. Instantaneously these lines darted into my mind:

> Would you the purple should your limbs adorn,
> Go wash the conscious blemish with a tear.

The man, who enjoys more pleasure in the mercenary embrace of a courtezan, than in relieving the unfortunate, is a detestable character, whatever his bright talents may be.

I pity him! Sylvander, all his fortune could not purchase half the luxury of Friday night! Let us be grateful to Heaven, though it has denied us wealth and power, for being endued with feelings, fitted to yield the most exquisite enjoyments here and hereafter! May I hope you'll read what I have urged on religion with attention, Sylvander! when Reason resumes her reign? I've none of these future delusive hopes, which you too vainly express as having towards Clarinda. Do not indulge them; my wishes extend to your immortal welfare. Let your first care be to please God: for that, which He delights in, must be happiness. I must conclude, or I'll relapse. I have not a grain of humour to-night in my composition; so, lest "charming Clarinda" should make you yawn, she'll decently say "good night!" I laugh to myself at the recollection of your earnest asseverations as to your being anti-Platonic! Want of passions is not merit: strong ones, under the control of reason and religion—let these be our glory.

Once more good night.

CLARINDA

## LETTER XXXVI

SYLVANDER TO CLARINDA
*Saturday Morning,* [*February 2d.*]

There is no time, my Clarinda, when the conscious thrilling chords of Love and Friendship give such delight, as in the pensive hours of what our favourite Thomson calls "philosophic melancholy." The sportive insects, who bask in the sunshine of Prosperity, or the worms, that luxuriant crawl amid their ample wealth of earth; they need no

Clarinda—they would despise Sylvander, if they dared. The family of Misfortune, a numerous group of brothers and sisters!—they need a resting-place to their souls. Unnoticed, often condemned by the world—in some degree, perhaps, condemned by themselves—they feel the full enjoyment of ardent love, delicate tender endearments, mutual esteem, and mutual reliance.

In this light, I have often admired religion. In proportion as we are wrung with grief, or distracted with anxiety, the ideas of a compassionate Deity, an Almighty Protector, are doubly dear.

> 'Tis this, my friend, that streaks our morning bright;
> 'Tis this that gilds the horrors of our night.

I have been this morning taking a peep through, as Young finely says, "the dark postern of time long elapsed;" and you will easily guess 'twas a rueful prospect: what a tissue of thoughtlessness, weakness, and folly! My life reminded me of a ruined temple: what strength, what proportion in some parts!—what unsightly gaps, what prostrate ruins in others! I kneeled down before the Father of Mercies, and said, "Father, I have sinned against Heaven, and in thy sight, and am no more worthy to be called thy son!" I rose eased and strengthened. I despise the superstition of a fanatic; but I love the religion of a man. "The future," said I to myself, "is still before me: there let me

> On reason build resolve—
> That column of true majesty in man!

I have difficulties many to encounter," said I; "but they are not absolutely insuperable:—and where is firmness of mind shown, but in exertion? Mere declamation is bombast rant. Besides, wherever I am, or in whatever situation I may be,

> —'Tis nought to me,
> Since God is ever present, ever felt,
> In the void waste as in the city full
> And where he vital breathes, there must be joy.

*Saturday Night, Half after Ten.*
What luxury of bliss I was enjoying this time yesternight! My ever dearest Clarinda, you have stolen away my soul: but you have refined, have exalted it; you have given it a stronger sense of virtue, and a stronger relish for piety. Clarinda, first of your sex! if ever I am

the veriest wretch on earth to forget you; if ever your lovely image is effaced from my soul,

> May I be lost, no eye to weep my end,
> And find no earth that's base enough to bury me!

What trifling silliness is the childish fondness of the every-day children of the world! 'Tis the unmeaning toying of the younglings of the fields and forests; but, where Sentiment and Fancy unite their sweets, where Taste and Delicacy refine, where Wit adds the flavour, and Good Sense gives strength and spirit to all; what a delicious draught is the hour of tender endearment! Beauty and Grace in the arms of Truth and Honour, in all the luxury of mutual love.

Clarinda, have you ever seen the picture realized? not in all its very richest colouring, but

> Hope, thou nurse of young Desire,
> Fair promiser of Joy.—

Last night, Clarinda, but for one slight shade, was the glorious picture—

> —Innocence
> Look'd gaily smiling on; while rosy Pleasure
> Hid young Desire amid her flowery wreath,
> And pour'd her cup luxuriant, mantling high,
> The sparkling, heavenly vintage—Love and Bliss!

Clarinda, when a poet and poetess of Nature's making—two of Nature's noblest productions!—when they drink together of the same cup of Love and Bliss, attempt not, ye coarser stuff of human nature! profanely to measure enjoyment ye never can know.

Good night, my dear Clarinda!

SYLVANDER

---

## LETTER XXXVII

### SYLVANDER TO CLARINDA

### [*4th February 1788.*]

\*   \*   \*   I am a discontented ghost, a perturbed spirit. Clarinda, if ever you forget Sylvander, may you be happy, but he will be miserable.

O, what a fool I am in love!—what an extravagant prodigal of affection! Why are your sex called the tender sex, when I never have met with one who can repay me in passion? They are either not so rich in love as I am, or they are niggards where I am lavish.

O Thou, whose I am, and whose are all my ways! Thou see'st me here, the hapless wreck of tides and tempests in my own bosom: do Thou direct to thyself that ardent love, for which I have so often sought a return, in vain, from my fellow-creatures! If Thy goodness has yet such a gift in store for me, as an equal return of affection from her who, Thou knowest, is dearer to me than life, do Thou bless and hallow our band of love and friendship; watch over us, in all our outgoings and incomings, for good; and may the tie that unites our hearts be strong and indissoluble as the thread of man's immortal life!

I am just going to take your Blackbird, the sweetest, I am sure, that ever sung, and prune its wings a little.

SYLVANDER

## LETTER XXXVIII

### SYLVANDER TO CLARINDA
[*February 5th.*]

I cannot go out to-day, my dearest love, without sending you half a line by way of a sin offering; but, believe me, 'twas the sin of igno-rance. Could you think that I intended to hurt you by anything I said yesternight? Nature has been too kind to you for your happiness, your delicacy, your sensibility. O why should such glorious qualifi-cations be the fruitful source of wo! You have "murdered sleep" to me last night. I went to bed impressed with an idea that you were unhappy; and every start I closed my eyes, busy Fancy painted you in such scenes of romantic misery, that I would almost be persuaded you are not well this morning

> —If I unwitting have offended,
> Impute it not,
> —But while we live
> But one short hour, perhaps, between us two
> Let there be peace.

If Mary is not gone by the time this reaches you, give her my best compliments. She is a charming girl, and highly worthy of the noblest love.

I send you a poem to read till I call on you this night, which will be about nine. I wish I could procure some potent spell, some fairy charm, that would protect from injury, or restore to rest that bosom chord, "tremblingly alive all o'er," on which hangs your peace of mind. I thought, vainly I fear thought, that the devotion of love, love strong as even you can feel, love guarded, invulnerably guarded by all the purity of virtue, and all the pride of honour,—I thought such a love might make you happy. Shall I be mistaken? I can no more, for hurry.

*Tuesday Morning.*

## LETTER XXXIX

CLARINDA TO SYLVANDER
*Thursday, Twelve, [February 7th.]*

I have been giving Mary a convoy; the day is a genial one. Mary is a happy woman to-day. Mrs Cockburn★[23] has seen her "Henry," and admired it vastly. She talked of you, told her she saw you, and that her lines even met your applause. Sylvander, I share in the joy of everyone; and am ready to "weep with those who weep," as well as "rejoice with those who rejoice." I wish all the human race well,— my heart throbs with the large ambitious wish to see them blest; yet I seem sometimes as if born to inflict misery. What a cordial evening we had last night! I only tremble at the ardent manner Mary talks of Sylvander! She knows where his affections lie, and is quite unconscious of the eagerness of her expressions. All night I could get no sleep for her admiration. I like her for it, and am proud of it; but I know how much violent admiration is akin to love.

I go out to dinner, and mean to leave this, in case of one from you to-day. Miss Chalmers's letters are charming. Why did not such a woman secure your heart?—O the caprice of human nature, to fix on impossibilities.

I am, however, happy you have such valuable friends. What a pity that those who will be most apt to feel your merit, will be probably among the number who have not the power of serving you! Sylvander, I never was ambitious; but of late I have wished for wealth, with an ardour unfelt before, to be able to say, "Be independent, thou dear

★Authoress of the beautiful song to the tune of "The Flowers of the Forest," beginning, "I've seen the smiling of Fortune beguiling."

friend of my heart!" What exquisite joy! Then "your head would be lifted up above your enemies." Oh, then, what little shuffling sneaking attentions!—shame upon the world! Wealth and power command its adulation, while real genius and worth, without these, are neglected and contemned.

> In nature's simplest habit clad,
> No wealth nor power had he;
> Genius and worth were all he had,
> But these were all to me.

Forgive my quoting my most favourite lines. You spoke of being here to-morrow evening. I believe you would be the first to tire of our society; but I tremble for censorious remarks: however, we must be sober in our hours. I am flat to-day—so adieu! I was not so cheerful last night as I wished. Forgive me. I am yours,

CLARINDA

## LETTER XL

SYLVANDER TO CLARINDA
*Friday Morning, 7 o'Clock, [February 8th.]*

Your fears for Mary are truly laughable. I suppose, my love, you and I showed her a scene which, perhaps, made her wish that she had a swain, and one who could love like me; and 'tis a thousand pities that so good a heart as hers should want an aim, an object. I am miserably stupid this morning. Yesterday I dined with a Baronet, and sat pretty late over the bottle. And "who hath wo—who hath sorrow? they that tarry long at the wine; they that go to seek mixed wine." Forgive me, likewise, a quotation from my favourite author. Solomon's knowledge of the world is very great. He may be looked on as the "Spectator" or "Adventurer" of his day: and it is, indeed, surprising what a sameness has ever been in human nature. The broken, but strongly characterizing hints, that the royal author gives us of the manners of the court of Jerusalem and country of Israel are, in their great outlines, the same pictures that London and England, Versailles and France exhibit some three thousand years later. The loves in the "Song of songs" are all in the spirit of Lady M. W. Montague, or Madame Ninon de l'Enclos; though, for my part, I dislike both the ancient and modern voluptuaries; and will dare to affirm, that such an attachment as mine to Clarinda, and such evenings as she and I have spent, are what these greatly respectable and deeply experienced Judges of Life and Love never dreamed of.

I shall be with you this evening between eight and nine, and shall keep as sober hours as you could wish. I am ever, my dear Madam, yours,

SYLVANDER

### LETTER XLI
SYLVANDER TO CLARINDA.
[*February 13th.*]

MY EVER DEAREST CLARINDA,—I make a numerous dinner-party wait me while I read yours★ and write this. Do not require that I should cease to love you, to adore you in my soul; 'tis to me impossible: your peace and happiness are to me dearer than my soul. Name the terms on which you wish to see me, to correspond with me, and you have them. I must love, pine, mourn, and adore in secret: this you must not deny me. You will ever be to me

> Dear as the light that visits those sad eyes,
> Dear as the ruddy drops that warm my heart.

I have not patience to read the Puritanic scrawl. Damned sophistry. Ye heavens, thou God of nature, thou Redeemer of mankind! ye look down with approving eyes on a passion inspired by the purest flame, and guarded by truth, delicacy, and honour; but the half-inch soul of an unfeeling, cold-blooded, pitiful Presbyterian bigot cannot forgive anything above his dungeon-bosom and foggy head.

Farewell! I'll be with you to-morrow evening; and be at rest in your mind. I will be yours in the way you think most to your happiness. I dare not proceed. I love, and will love you; and will, with joyous confidence, approach the throne of the Almighty Judge of men with your dear idea; and will despise the scum of sentiment, and the mist of sophistry.

SYLVANDER

★The letters of Clarinda referred to in this and the three following letters, were not found by the Editor among the papers of Mrs M'Lehose, when delivered to him.

## LETTER XLII

Sᴙʟᴠᴀɴᴅᴇʀ ᴛᴏ Cʟᴀʀɪɴᴅᴀ
*Wednesday, Midnight, [February 13th.]*

Mᴀᴅᴀᴍ—After a wretched day, I am preparing for a sleepless night. I am going to address myself to the Almighty Witness of my actions— some time, perhaps very soon, my Almighty Judge. I am not going to be the advocate of Passion: be Thou my inspirer and testimony, O God, as I plead the cause of truth!

I have read over your friend's haughty dictatorial letter:[24] you are only answerable to your God in such a matter. Who gave any fellow-creature of yours, (a fellow-creature incapable of being your judge, because not your peer,) a right to catechise, scold, undervalue, abuse, and insult, wantonly and unhumanly to insult you thus? I don't wish, not even wish to deceive you, Madam. The Searcher of hearts is my witness how dear you are to me; but though it were possible you could be still dearer to me, I would not even kiss your hand, at the expense of your conscience. Away with declamation! let us appeal to the bar of common sense. It is not mouthing everything sacred; it is not vague ranting assertions; it is not assuming, haughtily and in-sultingly assuming, the dictatorial language of a Roman Pontiff, that must dissolve a union like ours. Tell me, Madam, are you under the least shadow of an obligation to bestow your love, tenderness, caresses, affections, heart and soul, on Mr M'Lehose—the man who has repeatedly, habitually, and barbarously broken through every tie of duty, nature, or gratitude to you? The laws of your country indeed, for the most useful reasons of policy and sound government, have made your person inviolate; but are your heart and affections bound to one who gives not the least return of either to you? You cannot do it; it is not in the nature of things that you are bound to do it; the common feelings of humanity forbid it. Have you, then, a heart and affections which are no man's right? You have. It would be highly, ridiculously absurd to suppose the contrary. Tell me then, in the name of common sense, can it be wrong, is such a supposition compatible with the plainest ideas of right and wrong, that it is improper to bestow the heart and these affections on another—while that be-stowing is not in the smallest degree hurtful to your duty to God, to your children, to yourself, or to society at large?

This is the great test; the consequences let us see them. In a widowed, forlorn, lonely situation, with a bosom glowing with love and tenderness, yet so delicately situated that you cannot indulge these nobler feelings except you meet with a man who has a soul capable ★ ★ ★ ★ ★ ★ ★ ★ ★
★ ★ ★ ★ ★ ★ ★ ★ ★ ★ ★
★ ★ ★ ★ ★ ★ ★ ★ ★ ★ ★
★ ★ ★ ★ ★ ★ ★ ★ ★ ★ ★
★ ★ ★ ★ ★ ★ ★ ★ ★ ★ ★

## LETTER XLIII

### SYLVANDER TO CLARINDA
#### [*February 14th.*]

"I am distressed for thee, my brother Jonathan." I have suffered, Clarinda, from your letter. My soul was in arms at the sad perusal. I dreaded that I had acted wrong. If I have wronged you, God forgive me. But, Clarinda, be comforted. Let us raise the tone of our feelings a little higher and bolder. A fellow-creature who leaves us—who spurns us without just cause, though once our bosom friend—up with a little honest pride: let them go. How shall I comfort you, who am the cause of the injury? Can I wish that I had never seen you—that we had never met? No, I never will. But, have I thrown you friendless?—there is almost distraction in the thought. Father of mercies! Against Thee often have I sinned: through Thy grace I will endeavour to do so no more. She who Thou knowest is dearer to me than myself,—pour Thou the balm of peace into her past wounds, and hedge her about with Thy peculiar care, all her future days and nights. Strengthen her tender, noble mind firmly to suffer and magnanimously to bear. Make me worthy of that friendship, that love she honours me with. May my attachment to her be pure as devotion, and lasting as immortal life. O, Almighty Goodness, hear me! Be to her, at all times, particularly in the hour of distress or trial, a friend and comforter, a guide and guard.

> How are thy servants blest, O Lord,
> How sure is their defence!
> Eternal wisdom is their guide,
> Their help Omnipotence.

Forgive me, Clarinda, the injury I have done you. To-night I shall be with you, as indeed I shall be ill at ease till I see you.

SYLVANDER

## LETTER XLIV

SYLVANDER TO CLARINDA
*Two o'clock, [February 14th.]*

I just now received your first letter of yesterday, by the careless negligence of the penny post. Clarinda, matters are grown very serious with us: then seriously hear me, and hear me Heaven!

I met you, my dear Clarinda, by far the first of womankind, at least to me. I esteemed, I loved you at first sight, both of which attachments you have done me the honour to return. The longer I am acquainted with you, the more innate amiableness and worth I discover in you. You have suffered a loss, I confess, for my sake; but if the firmest, steadiest, warmest friendship; if every endeavour to be worthy of your friendship; if a love, strong as the ties of nature, and holy as the duties of religion; if all these can make anything like a compensation for the evil I have occasioned you; if they be worth your acceptance, or can in the least add to your enjoyments,—so help Sylvander, ye Powers above, in his hour of need, as he freely gives these all to Clarinda!

I esteem you, I love you, as a friend; I admire you, I love you, as a woman, beyond any one in all the circle of creation. I know I shall continue to esteem you, to love you, to pray for you, nay, to pray for myself for your sake.

Expect me at eight; and believe me to be ever, my dearest Madam, yours most entirely,

SYLVANDER

## LETTER XLV

SYLVANDER TO CLARINDA
*[February 15th.]*

When matters, my love, are desperate, we must put on a desperate face—

On reason build resolve,
That column of true majesty in man—

or, as the same author finely says in another place,

> Let thy soul spring up,
> And lay strong hold for help on him that made thee.

I am yours, Clarinda, for life. Never be discouraged at all this. Look forward: in a few weeks I shall be somewhere or other, out of the possibility of seeing you: till then, I shall write you often, but visit you seldom. Your fame, your welfare, your happiness, are dearer to me than any gratification whatever. Be comforted, my love! the present moment is the worst; the lenient hand of time is daily and hourly either lightening the burden, or making us insensible to the weight. None of these friends—I mean Mr —— and the other gentleman— can hurt your worldly support: and of their friendship, in a little time you will learn to be easy, and by and by to be happy without it. A decent means of livelihood in the world, an approving God, a peaceful conscience, and one firm trusty friend—can anybody that has these be said to be unhappy? These are yours.

To-morrow evening I shall be with you about eight, probably for the last time till I return to Edinburgh. In the meantime, should any of these two unlucky friends[25] question you respecting me, whether I am *the man*, I do not think they are entitled to any information. As to their jealousy and spying, I despise them.

Adieu, my dearest Madam!

SYLVANDER

## LETTER XLVI

SYLVANDER TO CLARINDA

GLASGOW, *Monday Evening, Nine o'clock,* [*February 18th.*]

The attraction of Love, I find, is in an inverse proportion to the attraction of the Newtonian philosophy. In the system of Sir Isaac, the nearer objects were to one another, the stronger was the attractive force. In my system, every milestone that marked my progress from Clarinda, awakened a keener pang of attachment to her. How do you feel, my love? Is your heart ill at ease? I fear it. God forbid that these persecutors should harass that peace, which is more precious to me than my own. Be assured I shall ever think on you, muse on you, and, in my moments of devotion pray for you. The hour that you are not in my thoughts, "be that hour darkness; let the shadows of death cover it; let it not be numbered in the hours of the day!"

> When I forget the darling theme,
> Be my tongue mute! my fancy paint no more!
> And, dead to joy, forget my heart to beat!

I have just met with my old friend, the ship Captain★—guess my pleasure; to meet you could alone have given me more. My brother William, too, the young saddler, has come to Glasgow to meet me; and here are we three spending the evening.

I arrived here too late to write by post; but I'll wrap half-a-dozen sheets of blank paper together, and send it by the Fly, under the name of a parcel. You shall hear from me next post town. I would write you a longer letter, but for the present circumstances of my friend.

Adieu, my Clarinda! I am just going to propose your health by way of grace-drink.

SYLVANDER

---

## LETTER XLVII
### CLARINDA TO SYLVANDER
EDINBURGH, *Tuesday Evening, Nine o'clock,* [*19th February.*]

Mr —— has just left me, after half an hour's most pathetic conversation. I told him of the usage I had met with on Sunday night, which he condemned much as unmanly and ungenerous. I expressed my thanks for his call; but he told me, it "was merely to hide the change in his friendship from the world." Think how I was mortified: I was, indeed; and affected so, as hardly to restrain tears. He did not name you; but spoke in terms that showed plainly he knew. Would to God he knew my Sylvander as I do! then might I hope to retain his friendship still; but I have made my choice, and you alone can ever make me repent it. Yet, while I live, I must regret the loss of such a man's friendship. My dear, generous friend of my soul does so too. I love him for it! Yesterday I thought of you, and went over to Miss Nimmo, to have the luxury of talking of you. She was most kind; and praised you more than ever, as a man of worth, honour, genius.

★Mr Richard Brown, alluded to in the Poet's autobiography "as a very noble character, but a hapless son of Misfortune," whose acquaintance he had formed at Irvine.

Oh, how I could have listened to her for ever! She says, she is afraid our attachment will be lasting. I stayed tea, was asked kindly, and did not choose to refuse, as I stayed last time when you were of the party. I wish you were here to-night to comfort me. I feel hurt and depressed; but to-morrow I hope for a cordial from your dear hand! I must bid you good night. Remember your Clarinda. Every blessing be yours!

Your letter this moment. Why did you write before to-day? Thank you for it. I figure your heartfelt enjoyment last night. Oh, to have been of the party! Where was it? I'd like to know the very spot. My head aches so I can't write more; but I have kissed your dear lines over and over. Adieu! I'll finish this to-morrow.

Your CLARINDA.

*Wednesday, Eleven.*

Mary was at my bedside by eight this morning. We had much chat about you. She is an affectionate, faithful soul. She tells me her defence of you was so warm, in a large company where you were blamed for some trivial affair, that she left them impressed with the idea of her being in love. She laughs, and says, "'tis pity to have the skaith, and nothing for her pains."

My spirits are greatly better to-day. I am a little anxious about Willie: his leg is to be lanced this day, and I shall be fluttered till the operation is fairly over. Mr Wood thinks he will soon get well, when the matter lodged in it is discussed. God grant it! Oh, how can I ever be ungrateful to that good Providence, who has blest me with so many undeserved mercies, and saved me often from the ruin I courted! The heart that feels its continual dependence on the Almighty, is bound to keep His laws by a tie stronger and tenderer than any human obligation. The feeling of Honour is a noble and powerful one; but can we be honourable to a fellow-creature, and basely unmindful of our Bountiful Benefactor, to whom we are indebted for life and all its blessings; and even for those very distinguishing qualities, Honour, Genius, and Benevolence?

I am sure you enter into these ideas; did you think with me in all points I should be too happy; but I'll be silent. I may wish, and pray, but you shall never again accuse me of presumption. My dear, I write you this to Mauchline, to be waiting you. I hope, nay I am sure, 'twill be welcome.

You are an extravagant prodigal in more essential things than affection. To-day's post would have brought me yours and saved you sixpence. However, it pleased me to know that, though absent in body, "you were present with me in spirit."

Do you know a Miss Nelly Hamilton in Ayr, daughter to a Captain John H. of the Excise cutter? I staid with her at Kailzie, and love her. She is a dear, amiable, romantic girl. I wish much to write to her, and will enclose it for you to deliver, personally, if agreeable. She raved about your poems in summer, and wished to be acquainted. Let me know if you have any objections. She is an intimate of Miss Nimmo, too. I think the streets look deserted-like since Monday; and there's a certain insipidity in good kind of folks I once enjoyed not a little. You, who are a casuist, explain these deep enigmas. Miss Wardrobe supped here on Monday. She once named you, which kept me from falling asleep. I drank your health in a glass of ale—as the lasses do at Hallowe'en,—"in to mysel."

Happy Sylvander! to meet with the dear charities of brother, sister, parent! whilst I have none of these, and belong to nobody. Yes, I have my children, and my heart's friend, Sylvander—the only one I have ever found capable of that nameless, delicate attachment, which none but noble, romantic minds can comprehend. I envy you the Captain's society. Don't tell him of the "Iron Chain," lest he call us both fools. I saw the happy trio in my mind's eye. So absence increases your fondness: 'tis ever so in great souls. Let the poor wordlings enjoy (possess, I mean, for they can't enjoy) their golden dish; we have each of us an estate, derived from the Father of the Universe, into whose hands I trust we'll return it, cultivated, so as to prove an inexhaustible treasure through the endless ages of eternity

*Afternoon.*

Mr Wood has not come, so the affair is not over. I hesitate about sending this till I hear further; but I think you said you'd be at M. on Thursday: at any rate you'll get this on your arrival.

Farewell! may you ever abide under the shadow of the Almighty. Yours,

CLARINDA.

## LETTER XLVIII

SYLVANDER TO CLARINDA
KILMARNOCK, *Friday,* [*22d February.*]

I wrote you, my dear Madam, the moment I alighted in Glasgow. Since then I have not had opportunity: for in Paisley, where I arrived next day, my worthy, wise friend Mr Pattison did not allow me a moment's respite. I was there ten hours; during which time I was introduced to nine men worth six thousands; five men worth ten thousands; his brother, richly worth twenty thousands; and a young weaver, who will have thirty thousands good when his father, who has no more children than the said weaver, and a Whig-kirk, dies. Mr P. was bred a zealous Antiburgher; but, during his widowerhood, he has found their strictness incompatible with certain compromises he is often obliged to make with those Powers of darkness—the devil, the world, and the flesh: so he, good, merciful man! talked privately to me of the absurdity of eternal torments; the liberality of sentiment in indulging the honest instincts of nature; the mysteries of ★ ★ ★ &c. He has a son, however, that, at sixteen, has repeatedly minted★ at certain privileges, only proper for sober, staid men, who can use the good things of this life without abusing them; but the father's parental vigilance has hitherto hedged him in, amid a corrupt and evil world.

His only daughter, who, "if the beast be to the fore, and the branks bide hale," will have seven thousand pounds when her old father steps into the dark Factory-office of Eternity with his well-thummed web of life, has put him again and again in a commendable fit of indignation, by requesting a harpsichord. "O! these boarding-schools!" exclaims my prudent friend. "She was a good spinner and sewer, till I was advised by her foes and mine to give her a year of Edinburgh!"

After two bottles more, my much-respected friend opened up to me a project, a legitimate child of Wisdom and Good Sense; 'twas no less than a long thought-on and deeply-matured design, to marry a girl, fully as elegant in her form as the famous priestess whom Saul consulted in his last hours, and who had been second maid of honour to his deceased wife. This, you may be sure, I highly applauded, so I hope for a pair of gloves by and by. I spent the two bypast days at Dunlop House with that worthy family to whom I was deeply

★*Anglicè*—Aimed at, attempted.

72

indebted early in my poetic career; and in about two hours I shall present your "twa wee sarkies" to the little fellow.★[26] My dearest Clarinda, you are ever present with me; and these hours, that drawl by among the fools and rascals of this world, are only supportable in the idea, that they are the forerunners of that happy hour, that ushers me to "the mistress of my soul." Next week I shall visit Dumfries, and next again return to Edinburgh. My letters, in these hurrying dissipated hours, will be heavy trash; but you know the writer.

God bless you.

SYLVANDER

## LETTER XLIX

CLARINDA TO SYLVANDER

EDINBURGH, *Friday Evening,* [*22d Feb.*]

I wish you had given me a hint, my dear Sylvander, that you were to write me only once in a week. Yesterday I looked for a letter; to-day, never doubted it; but both days have terminated in disappointment. A thousand conjectures have conspired to make me most unhappy. Often have I suffered much disquiet from forming the idea of such an attention, on such and such an occasion, and experienced quite the reverse. But in you, and you alone, I have ever found my highest demands of kindness accomplished; nay, even my fondest wishes, not gratified only, but anticipated! To what, then, can I attribute your not writing me one line since Monday?

God forbid that your nervous ailment has incapacitated you for that office, from which you derived pleasure singly; as well as that most delicate of all enjoyments, pleasure reflected. To-morrow I shall hope to hear from you. Hope, blessed hope, thou balm of every wo, possess and fill my bosom with thy benign influence.

I have been solitary since the tender farewell till to-night. I was solicited to go to Dr Moyes's lecture with Miss Craig and a gallant of hers, a student; one of the many stupid animals, knowing only in the Science of Puppyism, "or the nice conduct of a clouded cane." With what sovereign contempt did I compare his trite, insipid frivolity, with the intelligent, manly observation which ever marks the conversation of Sylvander. He is a glorious piece of divine workmanship, Dr

★ See page [19].

Moyes. The subject to-night was the origin of minerals, springs, lakes, and the ocean. Many parts were far beyond my weak comprehension, and indeed that of most women. What I understood delighted me, and altogether raised my thoughts to the infinite wisdom and boundless goodness of the Deity. The man himself marks both. Presented with a universal blank of Nature's works,* his mind appears to be illuminated with Celestial light. He concluded with some lines of the Essay on Man: "All are but parts of one stupendous whole," &c.; a passage I have often read with sublime pleasure.

Miss Burnet† sat just behind me. What an angelic girl! I stared at her, having never seen her so near. I remembered you talking of her, &c. What felicity to witness her "Softly speak and sweetly smile!" How could you celebrate any other Clarinda! Oh, I would have adored you, as Pope of exquisite taste and refinement, had you loved, sighed, and written upon her for ever! breathing your passion only to the woods and streams. But Poets, I find, are not quite incorporeal, more than others. My dear Sylvander, to be serious, I really wonder you ever admired Clarinda, after beholding Miss Burnet's superior charms. If I don't hear to-morrow, I shall form dreadful reasons. God forbid! Bishop Geddes was within a foot of me, too. What field for contemplation—both!

Good night. God bless you, prays
CLARINDA.

### LETTER L

SYLVANDER TO CLARINDA
CUMNOCK, *2d March, 1788*

I hope, and am certain, that my generous Clarinda will not think my silence, for now a long week, has been in any degree owing to my forgetfulness. I have been tossed about through the country ever since I wrote you; and am here returning from Dumfries-shire, at an inn, the post-office of the place, with just so long time as my horse

---

*Dr Moyes was blind.
†This young lady died of consumption in 1790, at the age of twenty-five. She was second daughter of the eccentric Lord Monboddo, and refused several advantageous offers of marriage, to nurse his declining years. She was a rare combination of beauty, grace, and goodness.

eats his corn, to write you. I have been hurried with business and dissipation, almost equal to the insidious degree of the Persian monarch's mandate, when he forbade asking petition of God or man for forty days. Had the venerable prophet been as strong as I, he had not broken the decree; at least not thrice a-day.

I am thinking my farming scheme will yet hold. A worthy intelligent farmer, my father's friend and my own, has been with me on the spot: he thinks the bargain practicable. I am myself, on a more serious review of the lands, much better pleased with them. I won't mention this in writing to anybody but you and Mr Ainslie. Don't accuse me of being fickle; I have the two plans of life before me, and I wish to adopt the one most likely to procure me independence.

I shall be in Edinburgh next week. I long to see you; your image is omnipresent to me; nay, I am convinced I would soon idolatrize it most seriously; so much do absence and memory improve the medium through which one sees the much-loved object. To-night, at the sacred hour of eight, I expect to meet you, at the Throne of Grace. I hope, as I go home to-night, to find a letter from you at the post-office in Mauchline; I have just once seen that dear hand since I left Edinburgh; a letter, indeed, which much affected me. Tell me, first of womankind, will my warmest attachment, my sincerest friendship, my correspondence,—will they be any compensation for the sacrifices you make for my sake? If they will, they are yours. If I settle on the farm I propose, I am just a day and a half's ride from Edinburgh. We shall meet: don't you say, "Perhaps, too often!"

Farewell, my fair, my charming Poetess! May all good things ever attend you.

I am ever, my dearest Madam,

Yours,

SYLVANDER

## LETTER LI

CLARINDA TO SYLVANDER
EDINBURGH, *March 5, 1788*

I received yours from Cumnock about an hour ago; and to show you my good-nature, sit down to write to you immediately. I fear, Sylvander, you overvalue my generosity; for, believe me, it will be some time ere

I can cordially forgive you the pain your silence has caused me! Did you ever feel that sickness of heart which arises from "hope deferred"? That, the cruelest of pains, you have inflicted on me for eight days by-past. I hope I can make every reasonable allowance for the hurry of business and dissipation. Yet, had I been ever so engrossed, I should have found one hour out of the twenty-four to write you. No more of it: I accept of your apologies; but am hurt that any should have been necessary betwixt us on such a tender occasion.

I am happy that the farming scheme promises so well. There's no fickleness, my dear Sir, in changing for the better. I never liked the Excise for you; and feel a sensible pleasure in the hope of your becoming a sober, industrious farmer. My prayers, in this affair, are heard, I hope, so far: may they be answered completely! The distance is the only thing I regret; but, whatever tends to your welfare, overweighs all other considerations. I hope ere then to grow wiser, and to lie easy under weeks' silence. I had begun to think that you had fully experienced the truth of Sir Isaac's philosophy.

I have been under unspeakable obligations to your friend, Mr Ainslie. I had not a mortal to whom I could speak of your name but him. He has called often; and, by sympathy, not a little alleviated my anxiety. I tremble lest you should have devolved, what you used to term your "folly," upon Clarinda: more's the pity. 'Tis never graceful but on the male side; but I shall learn more wisdom in future. Example has often good effects.

I got both your letters from Kilmarnock and Mauchline, and would, perhaps, have written to you unbidden, had I known anything of the geography of the country; but I knew not whether you would return by Mauchline or not, nor could Mr Ainslie inform me. I have met with several little rubs, that hurt me the more that I had not a bosom to pour them into—

On some fond breast the feeling soul relies.

Mary I have not once set eyes on, since I wrote to you. Oh, that I should be formed susceptible of kindness, never, never to be fully, or, at least, habitually returned! "Trim," (said my Uncle Toby,) "I wish, Trim, I were dead."

Mr Ainslie called just now to tell me he had heard from you. You would see, by my last, how anxious I was, even then, to hear from you. 'Tis the first time I ever had reason to be so: I hope 'twill be the last. My thoughts were yours both Sunday nights at eight. Why should my letter have affected you? You know I count all things (Heaven excepted) but loss, that I may win and keep you. I supped at Mr Kemp's on Friday. Had you been an invisible spectator with what perfect ease I acquitted myself, you would have been pleased, highly pleased with me.

Interrupted by a visit from Miss R——. She was inquiring kindly for you. I delivered your compliments to her. She means (as you once said) all the kindness in the world, but she wants that "finer chord." Ah! Sylvander, happy, in my mind, are they who are void of it. Alas it too often thrills with anguish.

I hope you have not forgotten to kiss the little cherub for me. Give him fifty, and think Clarinda blessing him all the while. I pity his mother sincerely and wish a certain affair happily over. My Willie is in good health, except his leg, which confines him close since it was opened; and Mr Wood says it will be a very tedious affair. He has prescribed sea-bathing as soon as the season admits. I never see Miss Nimmo. Her indifference wounds me; but all these things make me fly to the Father of Mercies, who is the inexhaustible Fountain of all kindness. How could you ever mention "postages"?[27] I counted on a crown at least; and have only spent one poor shilling. If I had but a shilling in the world, you should have sixpence; nay, eightpence, if I could contrive to live on a groat. I am avaricious only in your letters; you are so, indeed. Farewell. Yours,

Clarinda.

## LETTER LII

Sylvander to Clarinda
*[6th March.]*

I own myself guilty, Clarinda: I should have written you last week. But when you recollect, my dearest Madam, that yours of this night's post, is only the third I have from you, and that this is the fifth or sixth I have sent to you, you will not reproach me, with a good grace, for unkindness. I have always some kind of idea, not to sit down to write a letter, except I have time, and possession of my faculties, so as to do some justice to my letter; which at present is rarely my situation. For instance, yesterday I dined at a friend's at some distance: the savage hospitality of this country spent me the most part of the night over the nauseous potion in the bowl. This day—sick—headache—low spirits—miserable—fasting, except for a draught of water or small beer. Now eight o'clock at night; only able to crawl ten minutes' walk into Mauchline, to wait the post, in the pleasurable hope of hearing from the mistress of my soul.

But truce with all this. When I sit down to write to you, all is happiness and peace. A hundred times a-day do I figure you before your taper,—your book or work laid aside as I get within the room. How happy have I been! and how little of that scantling portion of time, called the life of man, is sacred to happiness, much less transport.

I could moralize to-night, like a death's-head.

> O what is life, that thoughtless wish of all!
> A drop of honey in a draught of gall.

Nothing astonishes me more, when a little sickness clogs the wheels of life, than the thoughtless career we run in the hour of health. "None saith, where is God, my Maker, that giveth songs in the night: who teacheth us more knowledge than the beasts of the field, and more understanding than the fowls of the air?"

Give me, my Maker, to remember thee! Give me, to act up to the dignity of my nature! Give me, to feel "another's wo"; and continue with me that dear-loved friend that feels with mine!

The dignifying and dignified Consciousness of an honest man, and the well-grounded trust in approving Heaven, are two most substantial foundations of happiness.  ★    ★    ★    ★    ★
★    ★    ★    ★    ★    ★    ★    ★    ★    ★    ★

I could not have written a page to any mortal, except yourself. I'll write you by Sunday's post.

Adieu. Good night.

SYLVANDER.

## LETTER LIII

SYLVANDER TO CLARINDA
MOSSGIEL, *7th March, 1788.*

Clarinda, I have been so stung with your reproach for unkindness,—a sin so unlike me, a sin I detest more than a breach of the whole Decalogue, fifth, sixth, seventh, and ninth articles excepted,—that I believe I shall not rest in my grave about it, if I die before I see you. You have often allowed me the head to judge, and the heart to feel the influence of female excellence: was it not blasphemy, then, against your own charms, and against my feelings, to suppose that a short fortnight could abate my passion?

You, my love, may have your cares and anxieties to disturb you; but they are the usual occurrences of life. Your future views are fixed, and your mind in a settled routine. Could not you, my ever dearest Madam, make a little allowance for a man, after long absence, paying a short visit to a country full of friends, relations, and early intimates? Cannot you guess, my Clarinda, what thoughts, what cares, what anxious forebodings, hopes and fears, must crowd the breast of the man of keen sensibility, when no less is on the tapis than his aim, his employment, his very existence through future life?

To be overtopped in anything else, I can bear; but in the tests of generous love, I defy all mankind! not even to the tender, the fond, the loving Clarinda—she whose strength of attachment, whose melting soul, may vie with Eloisa and Sappho, not even she can overpay the affection she owes me!

Now that, not my apology, but my defence is made, I feel my soul respire more easily. I know you will go along with me in my justification: would to Heaven you could in my adoption, too! I mean an adoption beneath the stars—an adoption where I might revel in the immediate beams of

She the bright sun of all her sex.

I would not have you, my dear Madam, so much hurt at Miss N[immo]'s coldness. 'Tis placing yourself below her, an honour she by no means deserves. We ought, when we wish to be economists in happiness,—we ought, in the first place, to fix the standard of our own character ; and when, on full examination, we know where we stand, and how much ground we occupy, let us contend for it as property; and those who seem to doubt, or deny us what is justly ours, let us either pity their prejudices, or despise their judgment. I know, my dear, you will say, this is self-conceit; but I call it self-knowledge: the one is the overweening opinion of a fool, who fancies himself to be, what he wishes himself to be thought; the other is the honest justice that a man of sense, who has thoroughly examined the subject, owes to himself. Without this standard, this column in our own mind, we are perpetually at the mercy of the petulance, the mistakes, the prejudices, nay, the very weakness and wickedness of our fellow-creatures.

I urge this, my dear, both to confirm myself in the doctrine, which, I assure you, I sometimes need, and because I know, that this causes you often much disquiet. To return to Miss N——. She is, most certainly, a worthy soul; and equalled by very very few in goodness of heart. But can she boast more goodness of heart than Clarinda? Not even prejudice will dare to say so: for penetration and discernment, Clarinda sees far beyond her. To wit, Miss N—— dare make no pretence: to Clarinda's wit, scarce any of her sex dare make pretence. Personal charms, it would be ridiculous to run the parallel: and for conduct in life, Miss N—— was never called out, either much to do, or to suffer. Clarinda has been both; and has performed her part, where Miss N—— would have sunk at the bare idea.

Away, then, with these disquietudes! Let us pray with the honest weaver of Kilbarchan, "Lord send us a gude conceit o' oursel!" or in the words of the auld sang,

> Who does me disdain, I can scorn them again,
> And I'll never mind any such foes.

There is an error in the commerce of intimacy.

★　★　★　★　★　★　★　★　★　★　★
★　★　★　★　★　★　★　★　★　★　★
★　★　★　★　★　★　★　★　★　★　★

Happy is our lot, indeed, when we meet with an honest merchant, who is qualified to deal with us on our own terms; but that is a rarity: with almost everybody we must pocket our pearls, less or more; and learn, in the old Scots phrase, "To gie sic like as we get." For this reason, we should try to erect a kind of bank or storehouse in our own mind; or, as the Psalmist says, "We should commune with our own hearts, and be still." ★　★　★　★　★
★　★　★

I wrote you yesternight, which will reach you long before this can. I may write Mr Ainslie before I see him, but I am not sure.

Farewell! and remember

Sylvander.

## LETTER LIV

CLARINDA TO SYLVANDER
EDINBURGH, *8th March, 1788.*

I was agreeably surprised by your answer to mine of Wednesday coming this morning. I thought it always took two days, a letter from this to Mauchline, and did not expect yours sooner than Monday. This is the fifth from you, and the fourth time I am now writing you. I hate calculating diem: like some things, they don't do to be numbered. I wish you had written from Dumfries, as you promised; but I do not impute it to any cause but hurry of business, &c. I hope I shall never live to reproach you with unkindness. You never ought to put off till you "have time to do justice to your letters." I have sufficient memorials of your abilities in that way; and last week, two lines, to have said "How do ye, my Clarinda," would have saved me days and nights of cruel disquietude. "A word to the wise," you know. I know human nature better than to expect always fine flights of fancy, or exertions of genius, and feel in myself the effects of this "crazy mortal Coil," upon its glorious inhabitant. To-day, I have a clogging headache; but, however stupid, I know (at least I hope) a letter from your heart's friend will be acceptable. It will reach you to-morrow, I hope. Shocking custom! one can't entertain with hospitality, without taxing their guests with the consequences you mention.

Your reflections upon the effects which sickness has on our retrospect of ourselves, are noble. I see my Sylvander will be all I wish him, before he leaves this world. Do you remember what simple eulogium I pronounced on you, when Miss Nimmo asked, what I thought of you:—"He is ane of God's ain; but his time's no come yet." It was like a speech from your worthy mother,—whom I revere. She would have joined me with a heartfelt sigh, which none but mothers know. It is rather a bad picture of us, that we are most prone to call upon God in trouble. Ought not the daily blessings of health, peace, competence, friends,—ought not these to awaken our constant gratitude to the Giver of all? I imagine, that the heart which does not occasionally glow with filial love in the hours of prosperity, can hardly hope to feel much comfort in flying to God in the time of distress. O my dear Sylvander! that we may be enabled to set Him before us, as our witness, benefactor, and judge, at all times, and on all occasions!

In the name of wonder how could you spend ten hours with such a —— as Mr Pattison?[28] What a despicable character! Religion he knows only the name; none of her real votaries ever wished to make any such shameful compromises. But 'tis Scripture verified— the demon of avarice, his original devil, finding him empty, called other seven more impure spirits, and so completely infernalized him. Destitute of discernment to perceive your merit, or taste to relish it, my astonishment at his fondness of you, is only surpassed by your more than Puritanic patience in listening to his shocking nonsense! I hope you renewed his certificate. I was told, it was in a tattered condition some months ago, and that then he proposed putting it on parchment, by way of preserving it. Don't call me severe: I hate all who would turn the "Grace of God into licentiousness;" 'tis commonly the weaker part of mankind who attempt it.

Religion, Thou the soul of happiness.

Yesterday morning in bed I happened to think of you. I said to myself, "My bonnie Lizzie Baillie," &c., and laughed; but I felt a delicious swell of heart, and my eyes swam in tears. I know not if your sex ever feel this burst of affection; 'tis an emotion indescribable. You see I'm grown a fool since you left me. You know I was rational, when you first knew me, but I always grow more foolish, the farther I am from those I love; by and by I suppose I shall be insane altogether.

I am happy your little lamb is doing so well. Did you execute my commission? You had a great stock on hand; and, if any agreeable customers came in the way, you would dispose of some of them I fancy, hoping soon to be supplied with a fresh assortment. For my part I can truly say, I have had no demand. I really believe you have taught me dignity, which, partly through good nature, and partly by misfortune, had been too much laid aside; which now I never will part with. Why should I not keep it up? Admired, esteemed, beloved, by one of the first of mankind! Not all the wealth of Peru could have purchased these. Oh, Sylvander, I am great in my own eyes, when I think how high I am in your esteem! You have shown me the merit I possess; I knew it not before. Even Joseph trembled t'other day in my presence. "Husbands looked mild, and savages grew tame!" Love and cherish your friend Mr Ainslie. He is your friend indeed. I long for next week; happy days, I hope, yet await us.

When you meet young Beauties, think of Clarinda's affection—of her situation—of how much her happiness depends on you.

Farewell, till we meet. God be with you.

CLARINDA.

*P.S.*—Will you take the trouble to send for a small parcel left at Dunlop and Wilson's, Booksellers, Trongate, Glasgow, for me, and bring it with you in the Fly?

## LETTER LV

### SYLVANDER TO CLARINDA
*[31st March.]*

I will meet you to-morrow, Clarinda, as you appoint. My Excise affair is just concluded, and I have got my order for instructions: so far good. Wednesday night I am engaged to sup among some of the principals of the Excise: so can only make a call for you that evening; but next day, I stay to dine with one of the Commissioners, so cannot go till Friday morning.

Your hopes, your fears, your cares, my love, are mine; so don't mind them. I will take you in my hand through the dreary wilds of this world, and scare away the ravening bird or beast that would annoy you. I saw Mary in town today, and asked her if she had seen you. I shall certainly bespeak Mr Ainslie as you desire.

Excuse me, my dearest angel, this hurried scrawl and miserable paper; circumstances make both. Farewell till to-morrow.

SYLVANDER.

*Monday, Noon.*

## LETTER LVI

### SYLVANDER TO CLARINDA
*[8th April.]*

I am just hurrying away to wait on the Great Man,[29] Clarinda; but I have more respect to my own peace and happiness, than to set out without waiting on you; for my imagination, like a child's favourite bird, will fondly flutter along with this scrawl, till it perch on your bosom. I thank you for all the happiness you bestowed on me yesterday. The walk—delightful; the evening—rapture. Do not be uneasy to-day, Clarinda; forgive me. I am in rather better spirits to-day, though I had but an indifferent night. Care, anxiety, sat on my spirits; and all the cheerfulness of this morning is the fruit of some serious, important ideas that lie, in their realities, beyond "the dark and the narrow house," as Ossian, prince of poets, says. The Father of Mercies be with you, Clarinda! And every good thing attend you!

SYLVANDER.
*Tuesday Morning.*

## LETTER LVII

SYLVANDER TO CLARINDA
*Wednesday Morning,* [*9th April.*]

Clarinda, will that envious night-cap hinder you from appearing at the window as I pass? "Who is she that looketh forth as the morning; fair as the sun, clear as the moon, terrible as an army with banners?"

Do not accuse me of fond folly for this line; you know I am a cool lover. I mean by these presents greeting, to let you to wit, that arch-rascal, Creech,★[30] has not done my business yesternight, which has put off my leaving town till Monday morning. To-morrow, at eleven, I meet with him for the last time; just the hour I should have met far more agreeable company.

You will tell me this evening, whether you cannot make our hour of meeting to-morrow one o'clock. I have just now written Creech such a letter, that the very goose-feather in my hand shrunk back from the line, and seemed to say, "I exceedingly fear and quake!" I am forming ideal schemes of vengeance.

★    ★    ★    ★    ★    ★    ★    ★    ★    ★    ★

Adieu, and think on
SYLVANDER

★ This eminent bookseller, who published the second edition of Burns' poems, was a pleasant companion, but of penurious habits, and extremely dilatory in the settlement of accounts, though a man of considerable wealth. The Poet had liked him at first, but latterly chafed exceedingly under the delay which the publisher made in rendering payment.

## LETTER LVIII

Sylvander to Clarinda
*Friday, Nine o'clock, Night, [11th April.]*

I am just now come in, and have read your letter. The first thing I did, was to thank the Divine Disposer of events, that he has had such happiness in store for me as the connexion I have with you. Life, my Clarinda, is a weary, barren path; and wo be to him or her that ventures it alone! For me, I have my dearest partner of my soul: Clarinda and I will make out our pilgrimage together. Wherever I am, I shall constantly let her know how I go on, what I observe in the world around me, and what adventures I meet with. Will it please you, my love, to get, every week, or, at least, every fortnight, a packet, two or three sheets, full of remarks, nonsense, news, rhymes, and old songs?

Will you open, with satisfaction and delight, a letter from a man who loves you, who has loved you, and who will love you to death, through death, and for ever? Oh Clarinda! what do I owe to Heaven for blessing me with such a piece of exalted excellence as you! I call over your idea, as a miser counts over his treasure! Tell me, were you studious to please me last night? I am sure you did it to transport. How rich am I who have such a treasure as you! You know me; you know how to make me happy, and you do it most effectually. God bless you with

Long life, long youth, long pleasure, and a friend!

To-morrow night, according to your own direction, I shall watch the window: 'tis the star that guides me to paradise. The great relish to all is, that Honour, that Innocence, that Religion, are the witnesses and guarantees of our happiness. "The Lord God knoweth," and, perhaps, "Israel he shall know," my love and your merit. Adieu, Clarinda! I am going to remember you in my prayers.★

Sylvander

---

★Probably several letters written about this period are lost. During the month, which the poet spent in Edinburgh, after his visit to Ayrshire, more than four letters must have passed.

With the exception of Letter LXVII, none of the letters of Clarinda, after the Poet's departure, have come into possession of the Editor.

When Burns left Edinburgh in April 1788, he presented an elegant pair of

## LETTER LIX

⤳

### Sylvander to Clarinda
*March 9th, 1789.*

Madam,—The letter you wrote me to Heron's carried its own answer in its bosom; you forbade me to write you, unless I was willing to plead guilty to a certain indictment that you were pleased to bring against me. As I am convinced of my own innocence, and, though conscious of high imprudence and egregious folly, can lay my hand on my breast and attest the rectitude of my heart, you will pardon me, Madam, if I do not carry my complaisance so far, as humbly to acquiesce in the name of Villain, merely out of compliment to your opinion; much as I esteem your judgment, and warmly as I regard your worth.

I have already told you, and I again aver it, that, at the period of time alluded to, I was not under the smallest moral tie to Mrs B——; nor did I, nor could I then know, all the powerful circumstances that omnipotent necessity was busy laying in wait for me. When you call over the scenes that have passed between us, you will survey the conduct of an honest man, struggling successfully with temptations, the most powerful that ever beset humanity, and preserving untainted honour, in situations where the austerest virtue would have forgiven

---

drinking glasses to Clarinda, with the following verses. The glasses were carefully preserved by her, and often taken down from the open cupboard in her parlour, to show to strangers. They are now in possession of the Editor.

#### TO CLARINDA,
##### WITH A PRESENT OF A PAIR OF DRINKING GLASSES.

Fair Empress of the Poet's soul,
  And Queen of Poetesses,
Clarinda, take this little boon,
  This humble pair of glasses

And fill them high with generous juice,
  As generous as your mind,
And pledge me in the generous toast,
  "The whole of humankind!"

"To those who love us!" second fill,
  But not to those whom we love;
Lest we love those who love not us.
  A third, "To thee and me, love!"

a fall: situations that, I will dare to say, not a single individual of all his kind, even with half his sensibility and passion, could have encountered without ruin; and I leave you to guess, Madam, how such a man is likely to digest an accusation of perfidious treachery.

Was I to blame, Madam, in being the distracted victim of charms which, I affirm it, no man ever approached with impunity? Had I seen the least glimmering of hope that these charms could ever have been mine; or even had not iron necessity—But these are unavailing words.

I would have called on you when I was in town, indeed I could not have resisted it, but that Mr Ainslie told me, that you were determined to avoid your windows while I was in town, lest even a glance of me should occur in the street.

When I shall have regained your good opinion, perhaps I may venture to solicit your friendship; but, be that as it may, the first of her sex I ever knew shall always be the object of my warmest good wishes.

## LETTER LX

### SYLVANDER TO CLARINDA
*[Spring of 1791.]*

I have, indeed, been ill, Madam, this whole winter. An incessant headache, depression of spirits, and all the truly miserable consequences of a deranged nervous system, have made dreadful havoc of my health and peace. Add to all this, a line of life, into which I have lately entered, obliges me to ride, upon an average, at least two hundred miles every week. However, thank heaven I am now greatly better in my health.   ⋆   ⋆   ⋆   ⋆   ⋆   ⋆   ⋆

I cannot, will not, enter into extenuatory circumstances; else I could show you how my precipitate, headlong, unthinking conduct leagued, with a juncture of unlucky events, to thrust me out of a possibility of keeping the path of rectitude; to curse me, by an irreconcileable war between my duty and my nearest wishes, and to damn me with a choice only of different species of error and misconduct.

I dare not trust myself further with this subject. The following song is one of my latest productions; and I send it you as I would do anything else, because it pleases myself.

## MY LOVELY NANCY
TUNE—*The Quaker's Wife.*

### I.
THINE am I, my faithful fair,
　　Thine, my lovely Nancy;
Ev'ry pulse along my veins,
　　Ev'ry roving fancy.

### II.
To thy bosom lay my heart,
　　There to throb and languish:
Tho' despair had wrung its core,
　　That would heal its anguish.

### III.
Take away those rosy lips,
　　Rich with balmy treasure;
Turn away thine eyes of love,
　　Lest I die with pleasure.

### IV.
What is life when wanting love?
　　Night without a morning:
Luve's the cloudless summer sun,
　　Nature gay adorning.


## LETTER LXI

～

SYLVANDER TO CLARINDA
*[Autumn of 1791.]*

I have received both your last letters, Madam, and ought, and would have answered the first, long ago. But on what subject shall I write you? How can you except a correspondent should write you, when you declare that you mean to preserve his letters, with a view, sooner or later, to expose them on the pillory of derision, and the rack of criticism? This is gagging me completely, as to speaking the sentiments of my bosom; else, Madam, I could, perhaps, too truly

Join grief with grief, and echo sighs to thine!

I have perused your most beautiful, but most pathetic Poem: do not ask me how often, or with what emotions. You know that "I dare to *sin*, but not to *lie!*" Your verses wring the confession from my inmost soul, that—I will say it, expose it if you please—that I have, more than once in my life, been the victim of a damning conjuncture of circumstances; and that to me you must be ever

Dear as the light that visits those sad eyes.

I have just, since I had yours, composed the following stanzas. Let me know your opinion of them.

Sweet Sensibility, how charming,
  Thou, my Friend, canst truly tell;
But how Distress, with horrors arming,
  Thou, alas! hast known too well!

Fairest Flower, behold the lily,
  Blooming in the sunny ray;
Let the blast sweep o'er the valley,
  See it prostrate on the clay.

Hear the wood-lark charm the forest,
  Telling o'er his little joys;
But, alas! a prey the surest
  To each pirate of the skies.

Dearly bought the hidden treasure
  Finer feelings can bestow:
Cords that vibrate sweetest pleasure
  Thrill the deepest notes of wo.

I have one other piece in your taste; but I have just a snatch of time.

### LETTER LXII
CLARINDA TO SYLVANDER
[*November, 1791.*]

SIR,—I take the liberty of addressing a few lines in behalf of your old acquaintance, Jenny Clow, who, to all appearance, is at this moment dying. Obliged, from all the symptoms of a rapid decay, to quit her service, she is gone to a room almost without common necessaries, untended and unmourned. In circumstances so distressing, to whom can she so naturally look for aid as to the father of her child, the man for whose sake she has suffered many a sad and anxious night, shut from the world, with no other companions than guilt and solitude?

You have now an opportunity to evince you indeed possess these fine feelings you have delineated, so as to claim the just admiration of your country. I am convinced I need add nothing farther to persuade you to act as every consideration of humanity as well as gratitude must dictate. I am, Sir, your sincere well-wisher,

A.M.

## LETTER LXIII
### Sylvander to Clarinda
*Dumfries, 23d November, 1791.*

It is extremely difficult, my dear Madam, for me to deny a lady anything; but to a lady whom I regard with all the endearing epithets of respectful esteem and old friendship, how shall I find the language of refusal? I have, indeed, a shade of the lady, which I keep, and shall ever keep in the *sanctum sanctorum* of my most anxious care. That lady, though an unfortunate and irresistible conjuncture of circumstances has lost me her esteem, yet she shall be ever, to me

Dear as the ruddy drops that warm my heart.

I am rather anxious for her sake, as to her voyage. I pray God my fears may be groundless. By the way, I have this moment a letter from her, with a paragraph or two conceived in so stately a style, that I would not pardon it in any created being except herself; but, as the subject interests me much, I shall answer it to you, as I do not know her present address. I am sure she must have told you of a girl, a Jenny Clow, who had the misfortune to make me a father, with contrition I own it, contrary to the laws of our most excellent constitution, in our holy Presbyterian hierarchy.

Mrs M—— tells me a tale of the poor girl's distress that makes my very heart weep blood. I will trust that your goodness will apologize to your delicacy for me, when I beg of you, for Heaven's sake, to send a porter to the poor woman—Mrs M., it seems, knows where she is to be found—with five shillings in my name; and, as I shall be in Edinburgh on Tuesday first, for certain, make the poor wench leave a line for me, before Tuesday, at Mr Mackay's, White Hart Inn, Grassmarket, where I shall put up; and, before I am two hours in town, I shall see the poor girl, and try what is to be done for her relief. I would have taken my boy from her long ago, but she would never consent.

I shall do myself the very great pleasure to call for you when I come to town, and repay you the sum your goodness shall have advanced. ★ ★ ★ ★ ★ ★ ★ ★ ★
★ ★ and most obedient,

Robert Burns

## LETTER LXIV

Sylvander to Clarinda

### LAMENT OF MARY, QUEEN OF SCOTS

A BALLAD

#### I.

Now Nature hangs her mantle green
　　On every blooming tree,
And spreads her sheets o' daisies white
　　Out o'er the grassy lea;
Now Phœbus cheers the crystal streams,
　　And glads the azure skies;
But nought can glad the careful wight
　　That fast in durance lies.

#### II.

Now laverocks wake the merry morn,
　　Aloft on dewy wing;
The merle, in his noontide bower,
　　Makes a' the echoes ring;
The mavis mild wi' many a note
　　Sings drowsy day to rest:
In love and freedom they rejoice,
　　Wi' care nor thrall opprest.

#### III.

Now blooms the lily by the bank,
　　The primrose doun the brae
The hawthorn's budding in the glen,
　　And milk-white is the slae:
The meanest hind in fair Scotland
　　May rove thae sweets among;
But I, the Queen of a' Scotland,
　　Maun lie in prison strong.

#### IV.

I was the Queen o' bonny France,
　　Where happy I hae been;
Fu' lightly rose I on the morn,
　　As blithe lay doun at e'en:

And I'm the Sovereign of Scotland,
    And mony a traitor there!
Yet here I lie, in foreign bands
    And never-ending care.

### V.

But as for thee thou false woman,
    My sister and my fae,
Grim Vengeance yet shall whet a sword
    That thro' thy soul shall gae.
The weeping blood in woman's breast,
    Was never known to thee
Nor th' balm that draps on wounds of wae,
    Frae woman's pitying e'e.

### VI.

My son, my son, may kinder stars
    Upon thy fortune shine;
And may those pleasures gild thy reign,
    That ne'er would blink on mine!
Heaven shield thee frae thy mother's faes,
    Or turn their hearts to thee
And where thou meet'st thy mother's friend,
    Remember him for me.

### VII.

O, soon to me may summer suns,
    Nae mair light up the morn!
Nae mair, to me, the autumn winds
    Wave o'er the yellow corn!
But in the narrow house o' death
    Let winter o'er me rave;
And the next flowers that deck the spring
    Bloom on my peaceful grave!

Such, my dearest Clarinda, were the words of the amiable but unfortunate Mary. Misfortune seems to take a peculiar pleasure, in darting her arrows against "honest men and bonny lasses." Of this, you are too, too just a proof; but may your future fate be a bright exception to the remark! In the words of Hamlet,

Adieu, adieu, adieu! Remember me.

Sylvander.
Leadhills, *Thursday, Noon,* [*11th December, 1791.*]

## LETTER LXV

SYLVANDER TO CLARINDA
DUMFRIES, [*15th December, 1791.*]

I have some merit, my ever dearest of women, in attracting and se-
curing the heart of Clarinda. In her I met with the most accomplished
of all womankind, the first of all God's works; and yet I, even I, had
the good fortune to appear amiable in her sight.

By the by, this is the sixth letter that I have written you since I left
you; and if you were an ordinary being, as you are a creature very
extraordinary—an instance of what God Almighty in the plenitude
of his power, and the fulness of his goodness, can make!—I would
never forgive you for not answering my letters.

I have sent in your hair, a part of the parcel you gave me, with a
measure, to Mr Bruce the jeweller in Prince's Street, to get a ring
done for me. I have likewise sent in the verses On Sensibility altered
to

> Sensibility how charming,
> Dearest Nancy, thou canst tell, &c.,

to the Editor of the Scots Songs, of which you have three volumes,
to set to a most beautiful air; out of compliment to the first of women,
my ever-beloved, my ever-sacred Clarinda. I shall probably write
you to-morrow. In the meantime, from a man who is literally drunk,
accept and forgive!

R.B.

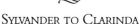

## LETTER LXVI

SYLVANDER TO CLARINDA
DUMFRIES, *27th December, 1791*

I have yours, my ever dearest Madam, this moment. I have just ten
minutes before the post goes; and these I shall employ in sending
you some songs I have just been composing to different tunes, for
the Collection of Songs, of which you have three volumes, and of
which you shall have the fourth.

## SONG

T<small>UNE</small>—*Rory Dall's Port*

Ae fond kiss, and then we sever;
Ae fareweel, and then for ever!
Deep in heart-wrung tears I'll pledge thee,
Warring sighs and groans I'll wage thee.

Who shall say that Fortune grieves him,
While the star of hope she leaves him?
Me, nae cheerful twinkle lights me;
Dark despair around benights me.

I'll ne'er blame my partial fancy,
Naething could resist my Nancy:
But to see her, was to love her;
Love but her, and love for ever.

Had we never loved sae kindly,
Had we never loved sae blindly!
Never met—or never parted,
We had ne'er been broken-hearted.

Fare-thee-weel, thou first and fairest!
Fare-thee-weel, thou best and dearest!
Thine be ilka joy and treasure,
Peace, Enjoyment, Love, and Pleasure!

Ae fond kiss, and then we sever;
Ae fareweel, alas, for ever!
Deep in heart-wrung tears I'll pledge thee,
Warring sighs and groans I'll wage thee.★

## SONG.

*To an old Scots Tune.*

Behold the hour, the boat, arrive!
   My dearest Nancy, O fareweel!
Sever'd frae thee, can I survive,
   Frae thee whom I hae loved sae weel?

★The fourth stanza Byron put at the head of his poem of the Bride of Abydos. Scott has remarked that it is worth a thousand romances; and Mrs Jameson has elegantly said, that not only are these lines what Scott says, "But in *themselves* a complete romance. They are," she adds, "the *alpha* and *omega* of feeling, and contain the essence of an existence of pain and pleasure, distilled into one burning drop."—*Chambers.*

Rory, or Roderick Dall, was a celebrated blind Highland harper. Port, in Gaelic, signifies a plaintive strain of music.

Endless and deep shall be my grief;
    Nae ray o' comfort shall I see;
But this most precious, dear belief!
    That thou wilt still remember me.

Alang the solitary shore,
    Where fleeting sea-fowl round me cry,
Across the rolling, dashing roar,
    I'll westward turn my wistful eye:

Happy, thou Indian grove, I'll say,
    Where now my Nancy's path shall be!
While thro' your sweets she holds her way,
    O tell me, does she muse on me!!!

### SONG
*To a charming plaintive Scots Air*

Ance mair I hail thee, thou gloomy December!
    Ance mair I hail thee wi' sorrow and care:
Sad was the parting thou mak'st me remember,
    Parting wi' Nancy, oh, ne'er to meet mair

Fond lovers' parting is sweet, painful pleasure,
    Hope beaming mild on the soft parting hour;
But the dire feeling, oh, farewell for ever
    Anguish unmingled and agony pure!

The rest of this song is on the wheels.★
Adieu. Adieu.
SYLVANDER

★The poet afterwards added the following verses:—

Wild as the winter now tearing the forest,
    Till the last leaf o' the summer is flown,
Such is the tempest has shaken my bosom,
    Since my last hope and last comfort is gone!

Still as I hail thee, thou gloomy December,
    Still shall I hail thee wi' sorrow and care;
For sad was the parting thou mak'st me remember,
    Parting wi' Nancy, oh, ne'er to meet mair!

# LETTER LXVII

~

### CLARINDA TO SYLVANDER
### *25th January, 1792.*

Agitated, hurried to death, I sit down to write a few lines to you, my ever dear, dear friend! We are ordered aboard on Saturday,—to sail on Sunday. And now, my dearest Sir, I have a few things to say to you, as the last advice of her, who could have lived or died with you! I am happy to know of your applying so steadily to the business you have engaged in; but, oh remember, this life is a short, passing scene! Seek God's favour,—keep His Commandments,—be solicitous to prepare for a happy eternity! There, I trust, we will meet, in perfect and never-ending bliss. Read my former letters attentively: let the religious tenets there expressed sink deep into your mind; meditate on them with candour, and your accurate judgment must be convinced that they accord with the words of Eternal Truth! Laugh no more at holy things, or holy men: remember, "without holiness, no man shall see God." Another thing, and I have done: as you value my peace, do not write me to Jamaica, until I let you know you may with safety. Write Mary often. She feels for you! and judges of your present feelings by her own. I am sure you will be happy to hear of my happiness: and I trust you will—soon. If there is time, you may drop me a line ere I go, to inform me if you get this, and another letter I wrote you, dated the 21st, which I am afraid of having been neglected to be put into the office.

So it was the Roselle you were to have gone in! I read your letter to-day, and reflected deeply on the ways of Heaven! To us they oft appear dark and doubtful; but let us do our duty faithfully, and sooner or later we will have our reward, because "the Lord God Omnipotent reigns:" every upright mind has here cause to rejoice. And now, adieu. May Almighty God bless you and yours! take you into His blessed favour here, and afterwards receive you into His glory!

Farewell. I will ever, ever remain

Your *real* friend,

A. M.⋆

———⤳

⋆Burns' thoughts often reverted to his fair friends and Edinburgh society. In February, 1792, Mrs M'Lehose sailed for Jamaica, about two months after the Poet's final interview with her. In the course of the ensuing summer, he bewailed her absence in the following pastoral:—

## LETTER LXVIII
## SYLVANDER TO CLARINDA.
### *[Autumn of 1792.]*

I suppose, my dear Madam, that by your neglecting to inform me of your arrival in Europe,—a circumstance that could not be indifferent to me, as, indeed, no occurrence relating to you can,—you meant to leave me to guess and gather that a correspondence I once had the honour and felicity to enjoy, is to be no more. Alas! what heavy-laden sounds are these—"No more!" The wretch who has never tasted pleasure, has never known wo; what drives the soul to madness, is the recollection of joys that are "no more!" But this is not language to the world: they do not understand it. But come, ye few,—the children of Feeling and Sentiment!—ye whose trembling bosom-chords ache to unutterable anguish, as recollection gushes on the heart—ye who are capable of an attachment, keen as the arrow of Death, and strong as the vigour of immortal being,—come! and your ears shall drink a tale—But, hush! I must not, can not tell it; agony is in the recollection, and frenzy in the recital!

But Madam,—to leave the paths that lead to madness,—I congratulate your friends on your return; and I hope that the precious

### MY NANNIE'S AWA'
Tune—*There'll never be peace, & c.*

#### I.
Now in her green mantle blithe Nature arrays,
And listens the lambkins that bleat o'er the braes,
While birds warble welcome in ilka green shaw;
But to me it's delightless—my Nannie's awa'.

#### II.
The snaw-drap and primrose our woodlands adorn,
And violets bathe in the weet o' the morn;
They pain my sad bosom, sae sweetly they blaw,
They mind me o' Nannie—and Nannie's awa'.

#### III
Thou laverock that springs frae the dews of the lawn,
The shepherd to warn o' the gray-breaking dawn;
And thou mellow mavis that hails the night fa',
Give over for pity—my Nannie's awa'.

#### IV.
Come autumn, sae pensive, in yellow and gray,
And soothe me with tidings o' Nature's decay:
The dark dreary winter and wild driving snaw
Alane can delight me—now Nannie's awa'!

health, which Miss P. tells me is so much injured, is restored, or restoring. There is a fatality attends Miss Peacock's correspondence and mine. Two of my letters, it seems, she never received; and her last came while I was in Ayrshire, was unfortunately mislaid, and only found about ten days or a fortnight ago, on removing a desk of drawers.

I present you a book: may I hope you will accept of it. I daresay you will have brought your books with you. The fourth volume of the Scots Songs is published; I will presume to send it you. Shall I hear from you? But first hear me. No cold language—no prudential documents: I despise advice, and scorn control. If you are not to write such language, such sentiments as you know I shall wish, shall delight to receive, I conjure you, by wounded pride! by ruined peace! by frantic, disappointed passion! by all the many ills that constitute that sum of human woes, a broken heart!!!—to me be silent for ever.

★ ★ ★ ★ ★ ★ ★ ★ ★ ★ ★
★ ★ ★ ★ ★ ★ ★ ★ ★ ★ ★
★ ★ ★ ★ ★ ★ ★ ★ ★ ★ ★
★ ★ ★ ★ ★ ★ ★ ★ ★ ★ ★

## LETTER LXIX

### Sylvander to Clarinda
[1793]

Before you ask me why I have not written you, first let me be informed by you, *how* I shall write you? "In friendship," you say; and I have many a time taken up my pen to try an epistle of "friendship" to you; but it will not do: 'tis like Jove grasping a pop-gun, after having wielded his thunder. When I take up the pen, recollection ruins me. Ah! my ever dearest Clarinda! Clarinda! What a host of memory's tenderest offspring crowd on my fancy at that sound! But I must not indulge that subject.—You have forbid it.

I am extremely happy to learn that your precious health is reëstablished, and that you are once more fit to enjoy that satisfaction in existence, which health alone can give us. My old friend Ainslie has indeed been kind to you. Tell him that I envy him the power of serving you. I had a letter from him a while ago, but it was so dry, so distant, so like a card to one of his clients, that I could scarce bear to read it, and have not yet answered it. He is a good honest friendly fellow, and can write a letter, which would do equal honour to his head and his heart, as a whole sheaf of his letters which I have by me will witness; and though Fame does not blow her trumpet at my approach *now*, as she did *then*, when he first honoured me with his friendship, yet I am as proud as ever; and when I am laid in my grave, I wish to be stretched at my full length, that I may occupy every inch of ground I have a right to.

You would laugh were you to see me where I am just now. Would to Heaven you were here to laugh with me, though I am afraid that crying would be our first employment. Here am I set, a solitary hermit, in the solitary room of a solitary inn, with a solitary bottle of wine by me, as grave and as stupid as an owl, but like that owl, still faithful to my old song; in confirmation of which, my dear Mrs Mac, here is your good health. May the hand-waled benisons o' Heaven bless your bonnie face; and the wratch wha skellies at your welfare, may the auld tinkler deil get him to clout his rotten heart! Amen.

You must know, my dearest Madam, that these now many years, wherever I am, in whatever company, when a married lady is called as a toast, I constantly give you; but, as your name has never passed my lips, even to my most intimate friend, I give you by the name of Mrs Mac. This is so well known among my acquaintances, that when any married lady is called for, the toastmaster will say—"O, we need not ask him who it is: here's Mrs Mac!" I have also, among my convivial friends, set on foot a round of toasts, which I call a round of Arcadian Shepherdesses; that is a round of favourite ladies, under female names celebrated in ancient song; and then you are my Clarinda. So, my lovely Clarinda, I devote this glass of wine to a most ardent wish for your happiness.

> In vain would Prudence, with decorous sneer,
> Point out a censuring world, and bid me fear:
> Above that world on wings of love I rise,
> I know its worst, and can that worst despise.

> "Wrong'd, injured, shunned, unpitied, unredrest;
> The mock'd quotation of the scorner's jest"—
> Let Prudence' direst bodements on me fall,
> Clarinda, rich reward! o'erpays them all.

I have been rhyming a little of late, but I do not know if they are worth postage.

Tell me what you think of the following monody.★

★    ★    ★    ★    ★

The subject of the foregoing is a woman of fashion in this country, with whom at one period I was well acquainted.[31] By some scandalous conduct to me, and two or three other gentlemen here as well as me, she steered so far to the north of my good opinion, that I have made her the theme of several ill-natured things. The following epigram★ struck me the other day as I passed her carriage.

★    ★    ★    ★    ★

★The Monody, Epitaph, and Epigram, which Burns lived to regret having written, are printed in his Works. [See Appendix VI.]

# APPENDIX I

~

## PREFACE TO THE 1843 EDITION

THE Correspondence of Burns and Clarinda has often been sought for, of late years, with the view of publication. Among others, Allan Cunningham, in the year 1834, when publishing his edition of the Life and Works of the Poet, made an unsuccessful application. Mrs M'Lehose, in a letter dated 16th July 1834, declined Mr Cunningham's request, and gave the following account of the original surreptitious appearance of a portion of the letters of Burns:—

"Mrs James Gray, then Miss Peacock, and Mr Grahame, the author of 'The Sabbath,' (two of my most valued and lamented friends,) applied to me on behalf of a literary gentleman of the name of Finlay, who was then engaged in writing a Life of the Poet, for permission to make *a few extracts* from the Letters to enrich his Life. This was unfortunately granted; and the Letters lent to Mr Finlay by Mr Grahame, under this express condition, that a few extracts inserted in the Life was the sole permission granted to him. Besides making this use of the Letters, Mr Finlay gave permission to a bookseller to publish all the Letters which had been intrusted to him, and added, most falsely, in an advertisement prefixed to them, that this was done with my permission, ('condescension,' as he termed it,) and that the editor was vested with the sole power to publish these Letters. Nothing could be more contrary to truth."

Allan Cunningham, when preparing the last volumes of his edition, wrote Mrs M'Lehose as follows:—"I am now arranging the materials for the remaining two volumes, and feel that I want your aid. Without the Letters of Clarinda, the works of Burns will be incomplete. I wish to publish them at the beginning of the eighth volume, with a short introduction, in which their scope and aim will be characterized. You will oblige me and delight your country by giving permission for this. I will do it with all due tenderness. I have a high respect for your character and talents, and wish you to reflect, that the world will in time have a full command over the Letters, and that ruder hands than mine will likely deal with them: my wish is for an opportunity to give an accredited edition of the Correspondence to the public, and give a right notion of their object and aim, while I have it so much in my power."

A reviewer, who was intimately acquainted with Clarinda for many years, in noticing Allan Cunningham's edition, thus writes:—"It is to be regretted that the letters to Clarinda are not embraced in this collection; but Mr Cunningham's explanation on this subject is quite satisfactory. We agree with him, that the letters in question are particularly valuable; and cannot but think that it is from some misapprehension, Clarinda has declined to sanction their publication. We are certain that they could have no such tendency as is feared; the justness of which opinion, we are sure, will at once be acknowledged by all who have the pleasure of knowing the estimable lady to whom they were addressed."

Mrs M'Lehose originally refused Mr Syme (who collected for Dr Currie) permission to publish the Letters; and declined, as has been already stated, various similar applications in her latter years. But the present editor is of opinion, that the time is now come for their publication, and that an authentic edition of the

Correspondence will have the effect of removing prejudice, will do honour to the memory of his respected relative, and interest the public, by giving them a new chapter in the life of our immortal poet. This interest, too, is increased by the consideration that these letters are probably the last original compositions of his which will ever be made public.

In reading the Correspondence of Burns and Clarinda, the reader will perceive, that several of *her* letters, and perhaps three or four of *his*, are wanting; and that, in those published, various passages are short-coming. A brief explanation, in relation to their custody, is therefore deemed necessary. This seems the more called for, when it is recollected that, in 1797, Clarinda wrote to Mr Syme, that she never would suffer one of them (the letters of Burns) to perish. Clarinda survived forty-four years; and it is perhaps a matter of surprise, that the Letters should have been so well preserved, and so few lost in such a long period.

In some of the Poet's letters, pieces have been cut out, to gratify (it is supposed) collectors of autographs, as it is well known that Mrs M'Lehose was much harassed with such applications: they are, besides, much torn, which was incidental to the frequent handling of them, for they were exhibited to gratify the curiosity of visiters. These are the sole causes of a few blanks being observable in the letters. The editor has an implicit belief that none were destroyed or suppressed by Mrs M'Lehose, or by her son the late Mr A. C. M'Lehose, W. S.

On the death of the latter, in April 1839, there was found in his repositories a bundle of papers, containing all the letters of Sylvander now published, and *a small portion of those of Clarinda.* These were taken possession of by Mr G. H. Pattison, advocate, on behalf of the editor, who was then resident abroad. Very soon after Mrs M'Lehose's death, a law-agent in this city, who acted for her under some sort of authority in the two years and a-half which intervened between her son's death and her own, removed from her repositories, which had been sealed up on the day of her funeral, *all her private papers.* The authority from Mrs M'Lehose, such as it was, came to an end by her death, and the removal of her papers was effected without warrant of any kind. Two boxes of these papers were delivered up to the editor, on his arrival in this country, in the spring of 1842; and, after some interval of time, several of Clarinda's letters were sent to him, with the apology, that they had *fallen out of a box or press.* It is curious that the only letters, which so fell out of a box or press, were several of Clarinda's letters to Burns, and the draft of a letter in which she declined sitting for her portrait for some of the poet's admirers.

The editor can only further express his belief, that Mr Pattison gave up to him the letters which he took charge of, in the same condition in which he found them in Mr M'Lehose's repositories and declare that he himself has given to the public all he received.

The editor takes this opportunity of rendering his best thanks to Mr Robert Chambers and Mr Pattison, for the useful suggestions which they have made, and the valuable assistance given in arranging the materials, and revising them for the press.

# APPENDIX II

## MEMOIR OF MRS M'LEHOSE BY HER GRANDSON W. C. M'LEHOSE

Mrs M'lehose, whose maiden name was Agnes Craig, was born in Glasgow in April 1759. She was the daughter of Mr Andrew Craig, surgeon in that city—a gentleman of a good family. His brother was the Rev. William Craig, one of the ministers of Glasgow, and father of Lord Craig, a Judge of the Court of Session. The mother of Mrs M'Lehose was a daughter of the Rev. John M'Laurin,—minister of Luss, and afterwards of St David's, Glasgow,—well known as the author of a volume of sermons; one of which, in particular, has always been viewed as a model of evangelical piety and pulpit eloquence. He was a brother of Colin M'Laurin, the celebrated mathematician and friend of Sir Isaac Newton.

Of the early years of Agnes Craig but little is recorded. She was so delicate in infancy, that it was hardly expected she would survive childhood. Yet, of four daughters and a son, she alone reached old age: all died in childhood except her sister Margaret, who, at the age of nineteen, became the wife of Captain Kennedy of Kailzie, and died about a year afterwards. The education of Agnes Craig was very incomplete,—as all female education was at that period, compared with the numerous advantages possessed by young people of both sexes in the present day. All the education bestowed upon her was some very imperfect instruction in English grammar, and that laborious idleness called sampler-work; even spelling was much neglected. The disadvantages attending such an education she afterwards fully perceived, and partially remedied at a period of life when many women neglect the attainments previously acquired, and but few persevere in the cultivation of further knowledge.

Agnes lost her mother when she was only eight years old; and her only surviving sister, Mrs Kennedy, dying about five years afterwards, she was deprived of that compensation for a mother's invaluable influence and superintendence which might have been derived from an elder sister's counsels. Her mother's instructions, however, were not lost upon her; for many years afterwards she referred with heartfelt gratitude to the benefit she derived from the religious principles instilled into her by her "sainted mother."

Henceforward, till her marriage, she lived with her father,—except that, for half a year, when fifteen years old, she was sent to an Edinburgh boarding-school—a practice apparently prevalent in those days as well as now—to finish that education which could not be said to have been properly begun, and had no solid foundation. This circumstance originated an acquaintance which ended in her marriage. Even at this early age, she was considered one of the beauties of Glasgow, and was styled "the pretty Miss Nancy." Mr James M'Lehose, a young man of respectable connexions, and a law agent in that city, had been disappointed in getting introduced to her ; and when he learned that she was going to Edinburgh, he engaged all the seats in the stage-coach excepting the one taken for her. At that period the coach took the whole day to perform the journey between the two cities, stopping a considerable time for dinner on the road, which thus afforded Mr M'Lehose an excellent opportunity of making himself agreeable,—an opportunity which he took the utmost pains to improve, and with great success, being possessed of an agreeable and attractive person, and most insinuating manners. His deficiency of sound principle was hidden from general observation by great plausibility. After the return of "the pretty Miss Nancy" to Glasgow, Mr M'Lehose followed up the acquaintance thus commenced, by paying her the most assiduous attention, and thus succeeded in winning her affections. Being young and inexperienced, deprived of the counsels of a mother and sister, and attached to one whom she thought possessed of every virtue, and who had shown so decided a partiality to her in a manner peculiarly calculated to please a romantic mind,—she favourably received his addresses.

In this she was not encouraged by her friends, who thought that her beauty, talents, and connexions, entitled her to a superior match. However, she became Mrs M'Lehose in July 1776, being then only seventeen years of age, and her husband five years her senior. Their union, she always stated, was the result of disinterested affection on both sides. But this connexion proved the bane of her happiness, and the source of all her misfortunes. Married at so early an age, before the vivacity of youth was passed, and, indeed, before it was fully developed, possessed of considerable personal attractions, a ready flow of wit, a keen relish for society, in which her conversational powers fitted her to excel, and a strong love of admiration, she appears to have displeased her husband, because she could not at once forego those enjoyments so natural to her time of life and situation. And he, without any cause, seems to have conceived the most unworthy jealousy, which led him to treat her with a severity most injudicious, and, to one of her disposition, productive of the worst consequences.

She soon discovered the mistaken estimate she had formed of her husband's character; and being of a high sanguine spirit, could ill brook the unmerited bad treatment she received. To use her own words, in a statement which she afterwards made for the advice of her friends—"Only a short time had elapsed ere I perceived, with inexpressible regret, that our dispositions, tempers, and sentiments, were so totally different, as to banish all hopes of happiness. Our disagreements rose to such a height, and my husband's treatment was so harsh, that it was thought advisable by my friends a separation should take place: which accordingly followed in December 1780."

Mrs M'Lehose had at this period only two children living—having lost her first born. A fourth was born a few months after this separation. Soon after this event, her husband took her infant children away from her, in the hopes of thereby working on her maternal feelings, and forcing a reunion which she had firmly refused, being convinced that they could not live happily together. She parted with her children with extreme reluctance—her father being both able and willing to maintain her and them; while her husband had neglected his business, and entered into every species of dissipation, so that he became unable to maintain his children, and they were distributed among his relations,—the youngest infant being, as soon as possible, removed from the tender care of his mother, and committed to the charge of a hireling nurse. He even prohibited her from seeing the children, to whom he knew she was devotedly attached. It required the utmost fortitude, on her part, to bear this cruel deprivation; but, by enduring it, she rendered her husband's cruel attempt abortive. All the children died young, except the late A. C. M'Lehose, W.S.

Immediately after the separation, she had returned to her father's house with her children, where she remained till his death, in the year 1782, two years afterwards.

He judiciously left his property to be invested in an annuity for her behoof, entirely independent of her husband, and beyond his control; and feeling it unpleasant to remain in the same city with her husband and his relations, and yet in a state of alienation, Mrs M'Lehose, by the advice of her friends, removed to Edinburgh in the same year, 1782.

Her husband followed her soon after, on his way to London, having formed an intention of going abroad. He solicited an interview in these terms—"Early to-morrow morning I leave this country for ever, and therefore wish much to pass one quarter of an hour with you. Upon my word of honour, my dearest Nancy, it is the last night you probably will ever have an opportunity of seeing me in this world." This appeal she refused for the following reasons:—"I consulted my friends: they advised me against seeing him; and as I thought it could be productive of no good, I declined the interview." The treatment she received from her husband while living with him, must have been bad indeed, to make one of her forgiving disposition so unyielding; and he seems to have been not altogether insensible to his misconduct: for, two years later, and just previous to going abroad he wrote to his wife— "For my own part, I am willing to forget what is past; neither do I require any apology from you: for I am heartily sorry for those instances of my behaviour to you which caused our separation. Were it possible to recall them, they should never be repeated." These feelings may have been sincere at the moment, but they had no depth or endurance.

Soon after Mr M'Lehose went to London, in the year 1782, he wrote his wife a very reproachful letter, stating his intention of going abroad, and bidding her take her children home to her. In this letter he observed—"The sooner you return to Glasgow the better, and take under your care and protection those endearing pledges of our once-happier days, as none of my friends will have anything to do with them." After speaking of his prospects of employment, he added—"Yet still, however remote my residence may be from you and those endearing infants, God forbid that I should be so destitute of natural affection for them, as to permit you or them, in the smallest degree, to be burdensome to any of your friends. On the contrary, I shall at all times observe the strictest economy, and exert myself to the uttermost, so that I may be enabled to contribute to your ease and happiness."

It will be seen in the sequel how this fair promise was observed. The truth is, that as he could not prevail on his wife to live with him, even by depriving her of her children to whom she was tenderly attached, and his relations would no longer support him in idleness, or his children for his sake, their sympathy for him being blunted, if not deadened, by his misconduct,—he thus contrived to throw the burden of them on his young wife, whose patrimonial income was very limited. Her situation at this trying period is thus related:—"The income left me by my father being barely sufficient to board myself, I was now distressed how to support my three infants. With my spirits sunk in deep dejection, I went to Glasgow to see them. I found arrears due for their board. This I paid; and the goodness of some worthy gentlemen in Glasgow procuring me a small annuity from the writers, and one from the surgeons, I again set out for Edinburgh with them in August 1782; and, by the strictest economy, made my little income go as far as possible. The deficiency was always supplied by some worthy benevolent friends, whose kindness no time can erase from my grateful heart."

When Mrs M'Lehose settled in Edinburgh in 1782, though comparatively a stranger, her youth, beauty, and misfortunes, and, above all, her exemplary conduct, procured for her the friendship, not only of her own relations, but of many respectable families, till then unknown to her, from whom she received many substantial proofs of kindness. Thus, though deprived of his assistance, to which she had the most sacred claim, she had much reason to bless God for his goodness in raising up so many friends. Among these friends, Lord Craig,★ her cousin-german, then an advocate at the Scottish bar, is particularly deserving of mention. He befriended her from her first arrival in Edinburgh, and continued, during his life, her greatest benefactor.

Mrs M'Lehose consulted him on all occasions of difficulty; and when deprived of the annuities from Glasgow, soon after her husband settled in Jamaica, on account of his ability to maintain his children himself, Lord Craig generously continued them, and made up the deficiencies of her income. At his death he left her an annuity. and made her son residuary legatee. Besides these substantial acts of kindness, she enjoyed his friendship, and was a frequent visitor at his house, where the best literary society of Edinburgh used to assemble.

During Mrs M'Lehose's early residence in Edinburgh, when she had not joined that social circle of which she soon became an ornament, she devoted much time and attention to remedying the defects of her early education. She improved her taste by the study of the best English authors, and became proficient in English composition. Possessed of a most retentive memory, she often quoted aptly from those authors, both in conversation and in her correspondence, which afterwards became extensive, and in which she excelled. It is to be regretted that so little of that correspondence has been preserved; but Mrs M'Lehose having survived nearly all the friends of her early life, applications made in quarters where it was supposed her letters might have been preserved, have been unsuccessful.

It was at this period, also, that Mrs M'Lehose began cultivating the Muses. She produced many short poetical effusions, a few of which have been preserved and are inserted in this volume. Her earliest composition was an "Address to a Blackbird," which she heard singing on a tree near her residence, in the neighbourhood of a spot where St Margaret's Convent has since been placed. The ideas, she stated, came into her mind like inspiration.

In the rearing and education of her children she took great delight; and the

---

★Lord Craig was the eldest son of the Rev. Dr Craig of Glasgow, and was born in the year 1745. He passed advocate in 1768; and after filling the offices of Depute-advocate and Sheriff-depute of Ayrshire, he was raised to the bench in 1792, and succeeded Lord Henderland as Lord Commissioner of Justiciary in 1795. He died in 1813.

The *Scots Magazine* of that year says of him, "As a judge he was highly honourable and upright—endowed with persevering talents and a complete knowledge of his profession. Few men despatched more business with greater precision than Lord Craig.

"When at the bar, though considered an able counsel, his practice never was extensive—he was rather remarkable as a man attached to the Belles Lettres. He wrote more papers in the *Mirror* and *Lounger* than any other contributor except Henry Mackenzie.

"In private life he was gentle, affable, and unassuming, and in an eminent degree hospitable and benevolent. He possessed the warm esteem of a select circle of friends, to whom he was extremely attached."

society of the many friends she acquired yielded her constant enjoyment for a long series of years, until the progress of time thinned their ranks, and increasing years and infirmities made her, in some degree, willing to relinquish social intercourse, of which she was so fond, for the retirement befitting old age. Among the literary men who used to visit her, Thomas Campbell, who was then prosecuting his studies at the University; the amiable Graham, the author of the "Sabbath;" James Gray, author of "Cuna of Cheyd," and"The Sabbath among the Mountains" and Robert Ainslie, the friend of Burns, author of various religious works addressed to the young, and of a series of political letters,—may be enumerated. This gentleman proved throughout life a warm and steady friend. He was an original visiter at Mrs M'Lehose's New-Year parties, which were kept up for about forty years, and are still remembered by several of the younger guests for their great conviviality, to which the liveliness and vivacity of the hostess greatly contributed.

Towards the end of the year 1787, Robert Burns was introduced to Mrs M'Lehose, in the house of a mutual friend, Miss Nimmo. They spent the evening together; and we have the sentiments recorded by both parties of the impressions reciprocally produced. The poet declared, in one of his letters to her, "Of all God's creatures I ever could approach in the beaten way of friendship, you struck me with the deepest, the strongest, the most permanent impression." While she wrote:— "Miss Nimmo can tell you how earnestly I had long pressed her to make us acquainted. I had a presentiment that we would derive pleasure from the society of each other." The poet was at this time preparing to depart from Edinburgh; and, under these circumstances, could only regret that he had not possessed the opportunity of cultivating the lady's acquaintance earlier; but a severe accident, which happened a day or two later, when he was engaged to spend the evening with her, delayed his departure for some time, and led to a correspondence, in which Mrs M'Lehose fancifully adopted the name of "Clarinda," and Burns followed up the idea by signing "Sylvander." As soon as he recovered from his accident, the poet visited the lady, and they enjoyed much of each other's society for several months, till he left Edinburgh. They met only once afterwards, in the year 1791,—but occasionally corresponded till within a short period of his death.

When Mr M'Lehose went to London in 1782, he found too many opportunities for indulging in dissipation and extravagance to go abroad so long as he was able to procure money from his family in Scotland,—assistance which they could ill afford, and were obliged, finally, to refuse, their patience and generosity being exhausted. After two years and a half thus spent in idleness, Mr M 'Lehose was thrown into prison for debt; and his relatives, being once more appealed to, consented to advance the funds necessary for his release and outfit, on condition that he immediately went abroad. With this he complied, and sailed for Jamaica, in November 1784. Before leaving London, and afterwards from Jamaica, where he became very prosperous, he wrote his mother and family most grateful letters for their kindness, but never repaid the debt, though appealed to, when his mother's income became inadequate to her support.

Mr M'Lehose did not favour his wife even with grateful letters; though she wrote him repeatedly respecting her circumstances and the health of their children. The following appeal to him, from Lord Craig, was equally fruitless:—"I write you this letter to represent to you the situation of your family here. Your wife's father left some property in Glasgow, the interest of which your wife draws for the support of herself and children; but this not being sufficient, by the solicitation of some of your friends £8 a-year was obtained from the surgeons, and £10 a-year from the writers in Glasgow. Even this, however, did not do, owing to the great rise in the expense of housekeeping, and the necessary outlay for your children, and their education; so that I advanced money to Mrs M., even while she got the above sums. Accounts, I am informed, have lately arrived from Jamaica which I am very glad of, representing you to be in a very good situation, and as having got into very profitable business. The surgeons and writers have withdrawn their allowance; and I have been told their principal reason for doing so, is the accounts they have heard of the goodness of your situation. No remittances, however, have, as yet, come from you; and in this last year, owing to the withdrawal of the writers and surgeons, I have paid Mrs M'Lehose upwards of £30 above what I have received. No person, except my brother, is willing to contribute anything; and all your own relations have positively refused, from the beginning, to contribute a single farthing. In this situation I am resolved to advance no more money out of my own funds on the account of your family. What I have already given, I have never laid my account in being reimbursed, and it shall never more be thought of; but for the future, every consideration demands that you should yourself contribute for the support of your own children. I expect, therefore, that you will, by the first opportunity, write to some of your correspondents in this country, giving what directions you think proper about your children, and making some proper remittance on their account; as, I repeat it again, I am determined not to continue to pay money on their account."

In Mrs M'Lehose's narrative she states:—"About the year 1787, my youngest boy William fell into ill health. This increased my expense; and, at this period, the annuities from Glasgow were withheld from me; the reason assigned being, that Mr M'Lehose was doing well, and in a way to support his children himself. I wrote once more to him, giving him an account of his children, particularly of William's helpless situation, and also my reduced circumstances, warmly expostulating with him on the duty and necessity of remitting for their support and education. I anxiously waited for an answer, but received none. In August 1790, my delicate child was happily delivered from his sufferings. I wrote again immediately of his death. Still I received no answer till the following August, when I had a letter, and, soon after, another, inviting me to come out to Jamaica, and enclosing a bill for £50, which was meant, I suppose, to equip me; and containing the most flattering directions to give his only surviving son the best education Edinburgh would afford."

"With regard to my dear son," Mr M'Lehose writes, "it is my wish that he should be placed in the first boarding-school for young gentlemen, either in Edinburgh or its environs: whatever expense may attend it, shall be regularly and punctually paid. It is my wish that he should continue at the Latin until he is perfect master of that language; and, when that is accomplished, I wish him to be instructed in the French, which is now become so generally useful all over the globe, and, in particular, here, where I intend to fix him in business. It will be proper, also, that he be immediately put under a dancing-master; and, what is still more requisite, that he should learn to fence. No expense can be incurred that will not be discharged with infinite pleasure and satisfaction, provided he is to benefit by it as I could wish. If you have no inclination to come out to this country, I then have to request you to embrace the first opportunity to inform me of such determination; as in that case I will immediately order my son up to London, and put him under the care of one of the first West India houses in the city, to receive the remainder of his education either at Westminster or at Eton, whichever they think most advisable."

Mrs M'Lehose was much at a loss how to act. At first she felt strongly inclined to remain in this country, but finally resolved to proceed to Jamaica. "I consulted my friends; they declined giving any advice, and referred me to my own mind. After much agitation, and deep and anxious reflection for my only child's sake, for whom he promised such liberal things, and encouraged by flattering accounts of his character and conduct in Jamaica, I resolved to undertake the arduous voyage."

The motives which influenced her will best be seen from the letter which she wrote to her friend Lord Craig, upon the subject. "When I wrote you last, the bidding adieu to my dear boy was my only source of anxiety. I had then no idea whatever of going out to Mr M'Lehose. Next day I learned from Mrs Adair that Captain Liddel told her my husband had the strongest resolution of using me kindly, in case I accepted of his invitation; and that pride alone hindered his acknowledging his faults a second time, still hurt at my not answering his overtures of reconciliation from London. But that, in case I did not choose to come over, I might rest assured I never would hear from him while he existed. Captain Liddel added his opinion, that I ought to go, in the strongest terms. Mrs Adair joins him; and, above all, my poor boy adds his entreaties most earnestly. I thought it prudent to inform him, for the first time, of the disagreement between his parents, and the unhappy jealousy in his father's temper. Still he argues that his father may be incensed at my refusal. If I go I have a terror of the sea, and no less of the climate; above all, the horror of again involving myself in misery in the midst of strangers, and almost without remedy. If I refuse, I must bid my only child (in whom all my affections and hopes are entirely centred) adieu for ever; struggle with a straitened income and the world's censure solitary and unprotected. The bright side of these alternatives is, that if I go, my husband's jealousy of temper may be abated, from a better knowledge of the world; and time and misfortunes, by making alterations both on person and vivacity, will render me less likely to incur his suspicions; and that ill humour, which partly arose from straitened fortune, will be removed by affluence. I will enjoy my son's society, and have him for a friend; and who knows what effect so fine a boy may have on a father long absent from his sight. If I refuse, and stay here, I shall continue to enjoy a circle of kind, respectable friends. Though my income be small, I can never be in want; and I shall maintain that liberty which, after nine years' enjoyment, I shall find it hard to forego, even to the degree to which I am sensible every married woman must submit."

A few days later she wrote again to the same gentleman. "On Friday last I went down to Leith, and had a conversation on board the Roselle with Captain Liddel. He told me that Mr M'Lehose had talked of me, and of my coming over, with great tenderness; and said, it would be my fault if we did not enjoy great happiness; and concluded with assuring me, if I were his own child he would advise me to go out. This conversation has tended greatly to decide my accepting my husband's invitation. I have done what you desired me,—weighed coolly (as coolly as a subject so interesting would permit) all I have to suffer or expect in either situation; and the result is, my going to Jamaica. This appears to me the preferable choice: it is surely the path of duty; and as such, I may look for the blessing of God to attend my endeavours for happiness with him who was the husband of my choice, and the father of my children. On Saturday I was agreeably surprised by a call from Mr Kemp. He had received my letter that morning at Glasgow, and had alighted for a few minutes, on his way to Easter Duddingston, where his family are for summer quarters. He was much affected with my perplexing situation. Like you, he knew not how to decide, and left me, promising to call early this day, which he has done. I told him of the meeting with Mr Liddel, and enumerated all the arguments which I had thought of on both sides of the question. What Mr Liddel (who is a man of known worth) said to me weighed much with him; and he, too, is now of opinion my going to Jamaica is advisable. He gave me much good advice as to my conduct towards Mr M'Lehose, and promised to write him himself. Your letter luckily arrived while he was with me. The assurance of my little income being secured me, not a little adds both to his opinion of the propriety of my going, and to my ease and comfort, in case (after doing all I can) it should prove impossible to enjoy that peace which I so earnestly pant after; and I would fain hope for a tender reception. After ten years' separation, and the sacrifice I make of bidding adieu (probably for ever) to my friends and my country—indeed, I am much depressed in mind—should I escape the sea, the climate may prove fatal to me; but should it happen so, I have the satisfaction to think I shall die in attempting to attain happiness in that path of duty which Providence and a succession of events seem to point out for the best. You, my dear kind benefactor, have had much trouble with me first and last: and though others appear ungrateful, neither time nor absence can ever erase from my heart the remembrance of your past kindness. My prayers shall ascend for the reward of heaven upon your head! To-morrow I am to write to my husband. Mr Kemp is to see it on Wednesday. If any person occurs to you as proper to place Andrew with in Edinburgh, let me know—the sooner the better: the hopes of his rejoining me will help to console my mind in the midst of strangers. I am sorry you are to be so long of coming to town. Meantime I shall be glad to hear from you: for I am, my dear Sir, in every possible situation, your affectionate and obliged friend, A. M."

"I accordingly wrote my husband in October 1791, acquainting him with my resolution of forgetting past differences, and throwing myself on his protection." As the Roselle did not leave for Jamaica till spring, she again wrote him in December. After giving the details of the arrangements she had made for their son's education, in compliance with his instructions, she thus proceeds:—"I had occasion to be in Glasgow lately for two days only. I called for your mother. I felt much for her— bereaved of so many children. The peculiar circumstances which attended poor Annie's death affected me excessively. They told me you had not written these three years past; but I assured them (and I hope it is the case) that your letters must have miscarried, as I could not believe you capable of such unkind neglect. I am certain, inclination, no less than duty, must ever prompt you to pay attention to your mother. She has met with many and sore afflictions; and I feel for her the most sincere sympathy." In the same letter, she adds:—"I have met with much kindness since I came to Edinburgh, from a set of most agreeable and respectable friends. No ideas of wealth or splendour could compensate for the pain I shall feel in bidding them adieu. Nothing could support me but the fond reliance I have of gaining your affections and confidence. To possess these is the dearest wish of my heart; and I trust the Almighty will grant this my ardent desire. I would fain hope to hear from you ere we sail; a kind letter from you would prove a balm to my soul during the anxieties of a tedious voyage."

Mrs M'Lehose sailed from Leith in February 1792, and arrived at Kingston in April following. The day before her departure she received a letter from her fickle husband, dissuading her from going out, on the pretence that the yellow fever prevailed in the island, and that a revolt had taken place among the negroes; both of which statements were false. But, having taken leave of her friends, engaged her passage, and made the preparations which the expectation of an absence, prolonged perhaps for years, required, she resolved (unwisely, as the event proved) to proceed. It is a curious coincidence that the vessel she sailed in was the "Roselle," the same in which Burns intended to have sailed for the same destination a few years earlier.

Mrs M'Lehose suffered much from the voyage, especially in the warmer latitudes; and when she reached Kingston, her husband did not go down to the ship for a length of time. All the other lady passengers had been speedily joined by their friends. When he came, he was very cold, and seemed far from being glad to see his wife; and even in this interview, before they left the ship, he used some harsh expressions towards her in presence of the captain and others, which wounded her feelings much.

"As my constitution never agreed with heat, I felt its bad effects as soon as we had crossed the Line; but the very cold reception I received from Mr M'Lehose on landing, gave me a shock which, joined to the climate, deranged my mind to such a degree as made me not answerable for what I either said or did. My husband's after-kindness could not remove the complication of nervous disorders which seized me. They increased to such a height that Dr Fife, the professional gentleman who attended me, and whose soothing manner I can never forget, was of opinion my going home was absolutely necessary—otherwise my reason, if not my life, would fall a sacrifice. Accordingly, in June I took leave of Mr M'Lehose, and returned home in the ship I had gone out in. Our parting was most affectionate. On my part, it was with sincere regret that my health obliged me to leave him. Upon his, it was to all appearance equally so. However, we parted with mutual promises of constancy, and of keeping up a regular correspondence. After getting into cool air, I gradually recovered in my health."

There were other reasons for leaving Jamaica besides those which she mentioned in the statement just quoted. Mr M'Lehose, like most West Indian planters, had a family by a coloured mistress. This could not be otherwise than a source of mortification and annoyance. The ebullition of temper which he had exhibited towards her on their first meeting, was a prelude to more violent outbreaks, which, though not always directed to her personally, paralyzed her with fear. His slaves were generally the objects of these fits of wrath; and seeing that his wife pitied their abject condition, he took pleasure in threatening and abusing them in her presence.

Circumstances were thus most unfavourable to Mrs M'Lehose's stay in Jamaica; but, had they been propitious, she was ill calculated to endure a permanent change of habits. That she was undoubtedly very unhappy in the West Indies, may be gathered from the following extract from her Journal many years afterwards:— "Recollect that I arrived in Jamaica this day twenty-two years. What I suffered during the three months I remained there! Lord make me grateful for thy goodness in bringing me back to my native country!"

Mrs M'Lehose arrived in Edinburgh in August 1792, and soon after resumed housekeeping, and took home her son, who had been placed at Dr Chapman's excellent boarding-school. The first year had now expired, without any part of the expense being defrayed by his father; and the debt was ultimately cancelled by the liberality of Lord Craig. As Mr M'Lehose continued thus utterly to neglect his wife and son, she was prevailed on by her friends to institute proceedings against him before the Court of Session, in order to enforce these obligations. In March 1797, accordingly, she obtained a judgment of the Court, ordaining him to pay her a yearly aliment of £100 sterling. From that judgment the following is an extract;— "In the close of the year 1784, Mr M'Lehose settled as an attorney-at-law, in Kingston, Jamaica; and business increased so rapidly, that he was soon in possession of, and still enjoys a revenue of £1000 a-year from his profession."

This decree, however, owing to Mr M'Lehose being resident in Jamaica, did not add to Mrs M'Lehose's income; although it was the means ultimately of enabling her to recover, in this country, some funds belonging to her husband.

Thus abandoned by her husband, Mrs M'Lehose and her only son, the late Mr Andrew M'Lehose, W.S., continued to live together. Soon after her return from Jamaica, Mr Robert Ainslie the friend of Burns, kindly took her son as apprentice. He continued to live with his mother until the year 1809, when he married. They lived most happily together; and probably there have been few instances of more devoted mutual attachment between parent and child.

In March 1812, Mr M'Lehose died at Kingston; and, though he had been in receipt of a large income for many years, as Chief Clerk of the Court of Common Pleas in Jamaica, no funds were ever received from that island by his family. A report reached this country, as being a matter of notoriety in Kingston, that some of his *particular friends* had, on the approach of death, sent all his domestics out of the house; and, as soon as the breath quitted his body, carried off whatever cash and documents there were. If so, the friends proved befitting the man. Notice, however, was given to Mrs M'Lehose that a balance of several hundred pounds, belonging to her husband, was in the hands of Messrs Coutts in London, which she soon afterwards obtained.

It was then discovered that he had had an account current at this bank for many years, while he had suffered his family to have their income eked out by the generosity of friends: £50 advanced to her, as already mentioned, before she sailed for Jamaica, and a present of £21 on leaving that island, being all which this wealthy husband bestowed on his family in the long period of thirty-two years. Yet, after her departure from Jamaica, he was in the habit of speaking of his family with great affection, and boasted of the valuable presents which he had made his wife and son. It is believed that few men have passed through life outwardly so respected by society, who have more basely neglected all the ties of affection and duty. He was a man of good talents and very pleasing address; much given to an ostentatious kind of hospitality. His temper was occasionally most violent and ungovernable; often soft and agreeable. His written correspondence with his wife partakes of the same character: the same letter containing alternate passages of the most endearing expressions and most insulting language.

Though Mrs M'Lehose survived her husband the long period of twenty-nine years, there are few or no incidents of any general interest in her after-life. Her best friend and benefactor, Lord Craig, died in 1813; and it was her fate not only to survive most of the friends of her middle life, but to see all her son's family, except one grandson, (the present editor,) pass away before her to the grave. Her son himself died suddenly in April 1839, having been predeceased by his wife and two children. After this event, Mrs M'Lehose's memory, which had begun to decline several years before, failed very much. Her other mental faculties were not so much affected, and her health and strength continued good,—so much so, that she was able to enjoy, till shortly before her death, her favourite walk round the Calton Hill. A lady, (widow of the late Commissary-general Moodie, of Van Diemen's Land,) who, with her sister, made the acquaintance of Mrs M'Lehose at a very late period of her life, and both of whom paid her much kind attention, has favoured the editor with some observations from her Journal, from which the following extracts are made:—

"*Edinburgh, 10th March, 1841.*—I have been interested by nothing more in this Queen of Cities, with its 'palaces and towers,' than by poor Burns' Monument. It is pleasant, in the land of his nativity, to find the bard of nature, and of all time, in full possession of that 'posthumous fame' which it was his delight to contemplate in life, and to which he was confident his genius would entitle him. An accidental circumstance, improved by my *curiosity,* (which I beg leave to dignify by denominating *literary,*) has brought me acquainted with one who was the friend and correspondent of the poet. This is the celebrated 'Clarinda,' who still lives, at the advanced age of eighty-two, near the Calton Hill. I have had many opportunities of conversing with her. Her memory is greatly impaired; and being also a little deaf, and seldom now quitting her house, common occurrences have ceased to interest her: even the affairs of the Kirk, which at present agitate and divide all Scotland from John o'Groat's to the Border, make no impression on her mind. But it is satisfactory to observe how much remains in that mind to cheer the hours of solitude, and to give consolation to the close of a life prolonged beyond the common lot.

"*30th March, 1841.*—Owing to sickness in my family I did not see Mrs M'Lehose for a short time. When I called, I found this interesting old lady much altered in appearance, though not in spirits. She lives in great simplicity, and is very sensible of the great blessing of health.

"*June, 1841.*—I still see her with interest; for, although her memory is much weakened by time, and the severe shock she suffered about two years ago in the sudden death of her son, yet her state is far from that of second childhood. She is perfectly conscious that her intellectual powers are much abridged. She remarked upon the loss of her memory,—'It was the strongest organ I possessed: therefore, having been so much exercised, it is no wonder it has taken leave the first.'

Although her memory is gone as to daily occurrences, yet her recollection is extraordinary as to past events, particularly in reciting anecdotes in verse in order to illustrate the conversation,—the subject of which she never misapprehends, whether lively or serious. Indeed, her mind is still the receptacle of fine thoughts,—and in conversation with *one* person, she is always ready, and never misapplies a quotation when the subject requires one. When there are many in the room, she becomes confused, and seems to take no part in the conversation; by reason, I think, of her deafness, more than any defect of understanding. Her piety is beautifully illustrated in her allusions to the Scriptures; and her memory is tenacious in reciting the Paraphrases. Speaking of old age, she observed 'on the loss each year sustains,' but she immediately added, as if recollecting that injustice might thereby be imputed to the Almighty,—

> He gives, and when He takes away
> He takes but what He gave.

She also quoted the tenth verse of the ninetieth Psalm, with great accuracy and emphasis. Even her conversation on religious subjects has been so entirely from the heart, that we have always enjoyed the subjects that led that way. She often expresses her thankfulness for the faithful attendance of her excellent servant, who is devoted to 'the mistress,' to whom she is now indebted for all her earthly comfort, and who is consequently much beloved and trusted by her."

"*22d October, 1841.*—Our old friend, Mrs M'Lehose, died this morning. She is gone, and I fully believe to her rest: for she was humble, and relied for acceptance upon the atonement. It has been a source of satisfaction to us to witness the composure of the last days of 'Clarinda.' To some who saw this old lady latterly, the apathy of age, and the loss of memory, gave the idea of greater feebleness of mind than was really the case. There were intervals in which she was still capable of a degree of mental exercise; and corresponding sentiments often served to elicit something of that mental activity for which she had been remarkable. We have frequently found her very collected and clear upon subjects which interested her. I had the blessing of prayer with her frequently; and on the day of her death I prayed by her bedside, but she could not join: she only pressed my hand, and said, 'I am much obliged to you.' She went off peacefully. Amongst her last words were, 'I go to Jesus.' 'When her faithful servant said to her, 'Do you fear death?' she answered, 'Not so much now.' After a short time she felt very cold, and, pressing her servant's hands, exclaimed, 'Margaret! Margaret!' and expired.

"I shall ever feel that my sister and myself have been highly favoured, in being considered by this old lady as a source of comfort in her last days, as her note to me, written ten days before her death, testifies. 'My dear Mrs Moodie, I am wearying to see you. Do give me a call. I am very poorly. I shall never forget your great kindness to me, and your being a stranger. I can give you no return, but my earnest wish that God may bless you and your little ones. May they be spared to you for a blessing, and at last may they be heirs of glory, is the wish amid prayers of your earnest friend, A. M. Oct. 12, 1841.' This was written in a firm, distinct hand."

Of Mrs M'Lehose's appearance in early life, it has already been recorded that she was considered one of the beauties of Glasgow. The editor's personal recollection does not extend beyond her middle life. She was short in stature; her hands and feet small and delicate; her skin fair, with a ruddy colour in her checks, which she retained to the end of her life; her eyes were lively, and evinced great vivacity; her teeth well formed, and beautifully white; her voice was soft and pleasing. Mrs M'Lehose's perceptive talents were not so good as her powers of reflection. Her judgment was often misled by her imagination, or biassed by the keenness of her feelings; but she read much; and having an excellent memory, and exercising sound reflection, she made the knowledge thus acquired her own. Her observation on the world around her was constant and acute, and she formed a true appreciation of her own position. But her sensitiveness was too great; her natural vivacity was strong, and when she gave full play to it in society, next day's reflection made her construe slight deviations, on her own part especially, and sometimes in others, into grave offences, for which she felt undue regret. She was very fond of society, and took a lead in it from her vivacity and ready wit; but when there were many strangers, she kept in the background. It seemed to require the fostering encouragement of those who had already shown an appreciation of her conversational powers to excite her to the exercise of them.

For thirty or forty years, it is believed she was in company five days out of seven; and when later years thinned the ranks of her friends, and diminished the number of her invitations, it was with great difficulty she became reconciled to a more re-tired mode of life. As her feelings were naturally strong, so were her attachments. She always considered ingratitude as one of the basest of sins. She would have been a devoted wife, had it not been her misfortune to be united to a man utterly in-capable of appreciating her, or of affording her happiness.

As a mother, she was fond and indulgent; and the only son who was spared to her, was the object of her warmest affections and most tender solicitude. Nor did her attachment to her friends cease with their lives. She cherished their memory when gone, and, in several instances, pays a tribute to their virtues, or the recollec-tion of former happy meetings, in her Journal, many years afterwards. As an exam-ple, her notices of Burns may be quoted:—

"*25th Jan., 1815.*—Burns' birth-day.—A great dinner at Oman's. Should like to be there, an invisible spectator of all said of that great genius."

"*6th Dec., 1831.*—This day I never can forget. Parted with Burns in the year 1791, never more to meet in this world.—Oh, may we meet in Heaven!"

Indeed, this habit Mrs M'Lehose indulged in to excess. It so happened that she had lost most of her relations in the month of March, which she therefore considered an unlucky month; and annually recorded the deaths, with such observations as show that she did not permit the soothing influence of time to efface the bitterness of past and unavailing sorrows.

# APPENDIX III

## INTRODUCTION TO THE CORRESPONDENCE OF SYLVANDER AND CLARINDA

Much misapprehension and prejudice seem to have prevailed respecting the nature of the acquaintance of Burns with Mrs M'Lehose. A portion of his letters having been surreptitiously printed many years ago,—in the absence of the lady's letters, which are now first published,—the worst construction was put on those passages which the Poet had written in moments of excitement or unguardedness. Yet the raptures, flights, and sentiments of two such minds, cannot be understood or ap-preciated without making allowances for their deviations from the ordinary track of commonplace intercourse. A glance at the various circumstances in the previous life of each, will show much that was calculated to attract the strongest mutual sympathies, in beings of so susceptible a nature.

To understand the line of propriety chalked out by the parties themselves, the feelings called forth by their occasional deviations from this self-prescribed boundary, and the caution observed by them—especially by the lady—as to their friends' and neighbours' opinions and surmises respecting their intercourse,—it is necessary to consider the relative situation of Burns and Clarinda at the period of their acquaintance, as well as the habits and manners of the time and place.

It was towards the close of the year 1787, when Burns had made up his mind immediately to leave Edinburgh, that he spent the evening with Mrs M'Lehose in the house of a mutual friend, in Alison Square, Potterrow. Powerfully impressed with the sprightly and intelligent character of the lady, he could, in these circumstances, only regret that he had not made her acquaintance at an earlier period; but an accident prevented his departure at the time he had appointed, which was afterwards still further delayed from other causes. During the tedious confinement occasioned by this accident, he cultivated the lady's acquaintance by correspondence; and, as soon as he was able to go out, visited her.

At this period, the first edition of his poems, published in Edinburgh, had been eminently successful,—producing considerable fame, and an amount of funds which, compared with his previous circumstances, must have seemed riches. He had been also introduced to circles of talent and acquirements, rank and fashion, which, in his original situation, he never could have hoped to see. But such unequal intercourse necessarily exposes the inferior to occasional caprice. Burns had some experience of this; and, as he always had a particular jealousy of people richer or higher than himself, he must have felt deeply mortified.

Again, with his ardent temperament, he could not but fall in love with some of the elegant young ladies he met with in these circles; and comparing their cultivated charms with those of his former loves, he seems to have felt a desire to possess one for a wife; but his inferior rank, unsettled circumstances, and, above all, his equivocal "certificate as a bachelor," presented an unsurmountable barrier. It is evident, that at this time he considered himself free of all legal and moral obligation to Jean Armour; regarding the burning of her marriage lines, and her acquiescence in their destruction, as releasing him from the responsibility of wedlock, though he felt "a miserable blank in his heart with the want of her."

Thus circumstanced, Burns made the acquaintance of Mrs M'Lehose; and is it to be wondered at, that he found great delight in the society of a lady of her talents and great vivacity,— well-read and fond of poetry, romantic, and a "bit of an enthusiast," warm in her feelings and attachments,—who immediately and keenly sympathized with him? or, is it a matter of surprise, that he felt, and sometimes expressed hopes that were wild and visionary?

Mrs M'Lehose was at this period a young married woman whose husband was abroad; but, owing to his unmerited bad treatment of her, a separation had taken place several years before. She was gifted with ardent affections, and feelings capable of the most devoted attachment,—in the prime of life,—not possessed of the "dear charities of brother, sister, parent:" for "I have none of these," she writes, "and belong to nobody." How deeply she felt the loneliness of her situation appears from what she writes in another letter:—"At this season, [New Year,] when others are joyous, I am the reverse. I have no *near* relations; and while others are with their friends, I sit alone, musing upon several of mine, with whom I used to be, now gone to the land of forgetfulness."

Thus as it were desolate, and feeling that "her heart—her fondest wishes— could not be placed on him who ought to have had them, but whose conduct had justly forfeited them,"—it was very natural, though not very prudent, that she had long "sought for a male friend…who could love me with tenderness—yet unmixed with selfishness; who could be my friend, companion, protector! and who would die sooner than injure me."

This friend she now found. "I sought, but I sought in vain. Heaven has, I hope, sent me this blessing in my Sylvander."

Though the friends of Mrs M'Lehose's husband condemned his conduct, and had suffered severely from it themselves, yet they, in some degree, espoused his cause; and no doubt were ready to listen to any whisper of slander against her. Her temperament, naturally too sensitive, led her to be extremely timid and cautious. Moreover, she had a young family, who needed all her care; and her circumstances being narrow, and eked out by the bounty of others, it behoved her to be guarded, lest imprudence might stop that bounty and throw her into increased difficulties.

Mrs M'Lehose was, in several respects, a ready mark for the ill-natured observations of the envious and censorious,—being a wit and a beauty, and having "an inveterate turn for social pleasure." When she indulged this turn, she admits that her vivacity often carried her too far. "If you saw me in a merry party, you would suppose me only an enthusiast in *fun*; but I now avoid such parties. My spirits are sunk for days after; and, what is worse, there are sometimes dull or malicious souls who censure me loudly for what their sluggish natures cannot comprehend. Were I possessed of an independent fortune, I would scorn their pitiful remarks; but everything in my situation renders prudence necessary."

When Burns visited Mrs M'Lehose, she lived in a court at the back of General's Entry, Potterrow, a narrow street into which this entry forms a passage. A small circular stair leads to the different floors, on the first of which she lived. The rooms are small and low-roofed, with windows of less size than many modern panes of glass.

In the year 1787, the building of the New Town of Edinburgh was not far advanced, and the good people were not accustomed to wide, airy streets; nor did they generally occupy spacious rooms, with abundance of the light of heaven. They were content to live in alleys and courts, or, at best, in narrow streets; and were satisfied with small rooms, with diminutive windows, which did not afford a sufficiency of daylight. When people lived in such close neighbourhood, they had much better opportunities than are afforded in the present day of watching the movements of their neighbours; opportunities which, it has been wickedly asserted, they were not slow to improve. To this they may have been so far incited by the deficiency of daylight; the very obscurity, perhaps, lending a charm to prying curiosity.

In Clarinda's letter to Sylvander, of the 16th January, there is an amusing instance of her anxiety to avoid this disagreeable sort of observation:—"Either to-morrow or Friday, I shall be happy to see you. …I hope you'll *come a-foot*, even though you take a chair home. A chair is so uncommon a thing in our neighbourhood, it is apt to raise speculation; but they are all asleep by ten." It is not to be doubted that a sedan chair would have caused much interesting speculation in an "entry;" and it was a lucky circumstance that the neighbours, some of whom, it is to be feared, were of the "coarser stuff of human nature," were such early-to-bed people.

When Mrs M'Lehose sought for a friend, who could love her with tenderness unmixed with selfishness, and found this friend in Sylvander, she underrated the influence of love and the power of the charmer. It is easy to resist the beginning of passion; easy to turn aside the stream when it is small; but difficult to direct or stem the current when the stream has become a torrent. Thus Clarinda became so rapidly and so strongly attached to Sylvander, that she herself trembled for the consequences. Pleased with the genius of this extraordinary man, who had "her best wishes before they met," she did not sufficiently estimate the danger of so tender an intercourse.

But though there were many rocks on which their love was threatened with ship-wreck, sometimes from the boldness of the pilot, sometimes from her own uncalled-for alarm, it is apparent that what she required in such a friend (and her requirements who shall condemn?) was satisfactorily fulfilled. "In you, and you alone, I have ever found my highest demands of kindness accomplished; nay, even my fondest wishes not gratified only, but anticipated." That Mrs M'Lehose was innocent of all criminal thoughts and intentions, it is believed no candid mind can doubt, after reading the following series of letters. Her love was, indeed, a flame "where innocence looked smiling on, and honour stood by, a sacred guard." Yet it may be doubted whether any married woman should have permitted herself to continue in circumstances of such temptation; certain it is, that few women could have come out of such a trial untarnished. But she did come forth unblemished, and live to a good old age, respected and beloved by all who knew her. This could not have been the case if there had been any spot in her character for scandal to point the finger at. Her attachment she had early revealed to her clergyman, and even taken his advice about it. It was a subject of conversation with various friends, some of whom even "trembled for her peace." Such frankness bears the stamp of conscious innocence.

It has been asserted, in the Life of Burns by Allan Cunningham, that "in general the raptures of Sylvander are artificial, and his sensibility assumed. He puts himself into strange postures and picturesque positions, and feels imaginary pains to corre-spond. He wounds himself, to show how readily the sores of love can be mended; and flogs his body like a devotee, to obtain the compassion of his patron saint." Similar views have been expressed by others; but surely they did not make allow-ances for a man of his ardent and enthusiastic nature. Besides, such opinions were formed upon a consideration of a portion only of *his* Letters, without any opportu-nity of perusing those of Clarinda. The tenor of the entire correspondence nega-tives such views, and shows that Sylvander took a decided interest in Clarinda from the first; that the feelings expressed by him were really felt, and not assumed: for no man can exhibit more earnestness and sincerity of purpose; and, indeed, he seems too soon to have hinted at hopes which were visionary. If Sylvander, at a later period, seriously entertained such hopes, it explains many of his strong expressions of attach-ment, otherwise bombastic. It must be admitted that several of his letters contain passages offensive from their boldness and presumption, which wounded the nice sensibility of Clarinda; but these were avowedly written after deep potations. His letters, in general, display his usual acute powers of observation, and are written in very various moods of mind.

It will be observed that matters are discussed in the letters, both of Sylvander and Clarinda, and seem to have formed the subject of conversation at their in-terviews, which the refinement of more modern times does not allow to be introduced—hardly alluded to. But it would not be fair to judge the manners of the last century by the standard of the present. The French Revolution, and the stirring events which followed, broke up the old order of things. The greatly-increased intercourse since the peace between Great Britain and the different nations of Europe, as well as between different sections of this country, together with the more general diffusion of literature and of a higher degree of cultivation, have had beneficial effects, quite incalculable, in eradicating the dissolute state of manners which prevailed during the last century, in removing local prejudices, and introducing increased refinement of taste, with more correct moral sentiments.

The visionary hopes entertained by the poet were generally checked by Clarinda, with a happy mixture of dignity and mildness, bespeaking inward purity. "Is it not too near an infringement of the sacred obligations of marriage, to bestow one's heart, wishes, and thoughts, upon another? Something in my soul whispers that it *approaches* criminality. I obey the voice; let me cast every kind feeling into the allowed bond of friendship. If 'tis accompanied with a shadow of a softer feeling, it shall be poured into the bosom of a merciful God! If a confession of my warmest, tenderest friendship does not satisfy you, *duty* forbids Clarinda should do more."

Yet it is evident she would not have been much distressed at a *circumstance* which would have "put it in the power of somebody (happy somebody) to divide her attention with all the delicacy and tenderness of an earthly attachment;" for she afterwards writes Sylvander,—"If I ever take a walk to the temple of H— [Hymen?] I'll disclose a cruel anguish of soul which I cannot tell you of; but you and I (were it even possible) would fall out by the way." Yet, oddly enough, a little later she writes to him:—"If she dare dispose of it [her heart,] last night can leave you at no loss to guess the man." Indeed, the decease of a worthless husband in a West India climate, happen when it might, could not have been a matter of surprise, any more than of regret.

Burns left Edinburgh about the middle of April 1788, to commence his farming operations in Nithsdale; and, ere long, he received from "Daddie Auld" his certificate as the husband of Jean Armour; but he had, soon after he reached Mauchline, privately acknowledged her as his wife. No letters of Burns and Mrs M'Lehose, between his departure and the 9th March 1789, are now extant. A serious quarrel seems to have taken place in this interval; and the cause may be easily inferred from his letter of that date. The lady was highly incensed; and friendship remained in abeyance till his visit to Edinburgh in November 1791. In a former visit to Edinburgh, the lady had refused to see him; but just previous to this—his last visit to the metropolis—she had written to him in behalf of a girl who had loved him not "wisely, but too well," and was then dying, and in want. In reply, he requested Mrs M'Lehose to relieve her necessities; and when he came to town he called to reimburse the trifling outlay which she had advanced, when a complete reconciliation seems to have taken place.

Occasional letters passed between them till within a short period of his death. Only one of hers remains, in which she takes an earnest farewell of him when about to leave for Jamaica in 1792. His letters betoken the altered circumstances and depressed spirits which characterized the latter years of his chequered life.

With two letters of Mrs M'Lehose to Mr Syme, who collected materials for Dr Currie when he was preparing his edition of Burns, these preliminary remarks will be brought to a close. They admirably illustrate the sprightly character of Clarinda, and contain some interesting observations respecting the immortal bard.

Extract of Letter.

Mrs M'lehose to Mr John Syme.

"What can have impressed such an idea upon you, as that I ever conceived the most distant intention to destroy these precious memorials of an acquaintance, the recollection of which would influence me were I to live till fourscore! Be assured I will never suffer one of them to perish. This I give you my solemn word of honour upon; —nay, more, on condition that you send me my letters, I will select such passages from our dear bard's letters as will do honour to his memory, and cannot hurt my own fame, even with the most rigid. His letters, however, are really not literary; they are the passionate effusions of an elegant mind—indeed, too tender to be exposed to any but the eye of a partial friend. Were the world composed of minds such as yours, it would be cruel even to bury them: but ah! how very few would understand, much less relish, such compositions! The bulk of mankind are strangers to the delicate refinements of superior minds."

Mrs M'lehose to Mr John Syme.

Edinburgh, *9th January, 1797.*★

"Dear Sir,—I am much obliged to you for the speedy return you made to my last letter. What could induce you to spend New Year's Day in so solitary a manner? Had I not heard *other things* of you, I should have imagined you in the predicament of Hamlet, when he exclaims, 'Man delights not me, nor woman neither.' I have a presentiment some *melancholy* recollection has been the cause of your secluding yourself from the world on a day when all ranks are devoted to festivity. When I first came to Edinburgh it was to me the dullest day in the year, because I had been accustomed to spend it in the society of several of the 'Charities,' as Milton styles them, who were no more. But, for several years past, I have acquired friends, with whom I pass it cheerfully, though death has deprived me of all near relations except Lord Craig, (my first cousin,) and a son, who is the pride and pleasure of my life. I thought a lady's letter, on a subject so near her heart, ought to have been answered— even had half an hour been stolen from your sleep, and therefore rallied you by a quotation from Lord Littleton's poem on Lucy pleading want of time: for the truth is, you were at a loss what to say; you wished not to return the letters, and hardly knew how to use the language of denial—is not this a just statement?

'For when a lady's in the case,
You know all other things give place.'

Seriously I can easily conceive you must be excessively hurried: twenty letters in a day—and dry uninteresting stuff! Had I them to write, they should be *favourites* indeed to whom I would add *one* to the *score*. I had no right to expect you to 'epistolize' to me, far less to be a regular correspondent. Your neglect of Mrs Riddell is amazing, because she is, in my estimation, the first female writer I ever saw; and, I am convinced, a good soul as ever was, from her uncommon attention to our dear B—— and his family. Besides, I suppose, she is an OLD FRIEND of yours. I am delighted with her letters, and reckon her correspondence a great acquisition. She sent me Mr Roscoe's Monody on Burns. She tells me 'tis he and Dr Currie are to be his editors. I am happy you have consented to return my letters at last, and that my pledge has pleased you. Please direct them, put up in a parcel, for my usual address, and send

★The Editor is indebted to Mr Robert Chambers for a copy of this Letter.

them by the Dumfries carrier, who comes here once a-week. You must pardon me for refusing to send B.'s. I never will. I am determined not to allow them to be out of my house; but it will be quite the same to you, as you shall see them all when you come to Edinburgh next month. Do write me previous to your arrival, and name the day, that I may be at home and guard against our being interrupted in perusing these dear memorials of our lamented friend. I hold them sacred—too sacred for the public eye; and I am sure you will agree they are so when you see them. If any argument could have prevailed on me, (and Mrs R. exhausted all her eloquence could dictate,) the idea of their affording pecuniary assistance was most likely. But I am convinced they would have added little to this effect: for I heard, by a literary conversation here, that it was thought by most people there would be too much intended to be published; and that letters especially it was nonsense to give, as few would be interested in them. This I thought strange, and so will a few enthusiastic admirers of our bard; but I fear 'tis the general voice of the public. I earnestly hope the MSS. may turn out as valuable as you suppose them. It rejoices me to hear so large a sum is to come from other places—and join you in reprobating Caledonia's capital for her shabby donation. But there are few souls *anywhere* who understood or could enter into the relish of such a character as B.'s. There was an electricity about him which could only touch or pervade a *few* cast in nature's finest mould. I fear I have been inaccurate, for I am hurried at present. You always shine when mounted on pigmies. I know not whether you may have reached the top of Parnassus; but you have certainly gathered some sweet flowers by the way.

"Yours with regard,

"CLARINDA."

# APPENDIX IV

## MRS M'LEHOSE'S FUGITIVE POETRY
*THE following fugitive Pieces are all that remain of the Poetry of Mrs M'Lehose.*

### TO A BLACKBIRD SINGING ON A TREE.
*Morningside*, 1784.

Go on, sweet bird, and soothe my care,
Thy cheerful notes will hush despair;
Thy tuneful warblings, void of art,
Thrill sweetly through my aching heart.
Now choose thy mate and fondly love,
And all the charming transport prove;
Those sweet emotions all enjoy,
Let Love and Song thy hours employ;
Whilst I, a love-lorn exile, live,
And rapture nor receive nor give.
Go on, sweet bird, and soothe my care,
Thy cheerful notes will hush despair.★

---

★Burns added four lines to this song, and having "pruned its [the Blackbird's] wings a little," (see Letter XXXVII,) inserted it in *Johnson's Musical Museum.*

## TO MR AINSLIE,

ON HIS LEAVING A VISITING CARD ON CHRISTMAS-DAY,
AFTER HAVING BEEN A GREAT STRANGER.
*Canongate,* 1790.

FULL many a Christmas have I seen,
But ne'er saw this before—
One's dear and always welcome friend
A card leave at the door.
Such ceremony sure bespeaks
A friendship in the wane:
Friendship, dear tie, when once it breaks,
Is seldom knit again.
Then fare-ye-well, my once dear friend,
And happy may you be;
May all your future hours be blest
Like those you've spent with me!

## EPITAPH ON MY GRANDCHILD'S CAT.

POOR Puss is dead! and William weeps,
Refuses food, and hardly sleeps,
Bemoaning o'er her early fate,
His blithe companion air and late.
Secure in his encircling arm,
He deemed her safe from every harm,
Frisking around him all the day,
In lively gambols, sport, and play;
At night when stretched on carpet-rug,
Could scarce resist his kindly tug.
Why, grisly Death, didst thou appear,
So soon to stop her gay career?
For she was sleekit, soft, and fair;
Grimalkin, sweet! of virtues rare!
Caress'd, alternate, by each boy,
Their morning care, their evening joy.
Now cold she lies! The youthful tear
Embalms poor Pussy's mournful bier.
But, dry your eyes, my lovely boys,
Life has for you a *store* of joys.

## ON THE LOSS OF MY CHILD, 1788.

DOES Heaven behold these sadly-falling tears,
Shed by a mother o'er her darling child?
Ah, blasted hopes! and heart-distracting fears,
That fill my breast with frantic sorrow wild!

Yes, Heaven beholds; from thence the stroke descends,
And Heaven alone can heal the wounds it gave.

Oh, Thou, who dost afflict for gracious ends,
  Lead my sad soul to scenes beyond the grave.

'Tis there alone all tears are wiped away;
  There death-divided friends shall part no more.
Oh, Thou Supreme! whose years know no delay,
  Teach me thy dispensations to adore.

### ON THE AUTUMN OF LIFE.

HAIL, pensive season! autumn of our days!
Though youth be past, and vivid pleasures o'er,
Thou showerest down thy precious fruits of wisdom,
Making us pause upon those mingled scenes
Of bliss and wo, that mark our passing state.
How oft the mind of sensibility
Recalls, in sadly-pleasing retrospect,
"The things that were," and must return no more;
The parents dear, who rear'd our early life;
The early friend, on whose fond breast we lean'd;
Or innocent, smiling babes, whose sweet endearments,
Twining around our hearts, have left a void,
Which nought but Heaven itself can e'er supply.
But, though our pleasing spring of life be past,
Autumn commenced, and winter full in view,
That sombre season to the feeling mind
Yields chastened joys to sprightly youth unknown:
Reflection's calm but solitary hours,
Passion subdued, and Friendship's tranquil joys.
The mind matured reviews her mental stores,
Her knowledge, high capacities, and powers—
Contemplates Nature in each varying form;
But chiefly human character in all
Its shades and wonderful diversities;
Soars to the great First Cause; beholds in Him
Wisdom supreme, and Goodness infinite;
Resigns the world, and leans, with confidence,
Upon the Rock of Ages.

### TO MR JAMES GRAY,
#### OF THE HIGH SCHOOL,
##### WHO HAD ASKED MY OPINION OF A BEAUTIFUL ODE HE HAD
##### JUST PUBLISHED, ALONG WITH MY LINES ON A LINNET,
##### WHICH HE HAD REQUESTED.

My dear Mr Gray, have patience, I pray,
  While perusing my poor little Linnet;
Though pretty it seem, 'tis a trifling theme,
  And you really will find little in it.

But your Ode so sublime, one Parnassus might dim
And yet not produce such another.
One blemish to find, I have puzzled my mind;
And, save one, it is good altogether.
Philosophers deem Life's joys all a dream;
But I ne'er heard its woes were eternal.
Bliss eternal above, we all hope to prove:
Leave the other to regions infernal.

## ON THE DEATH OF MRS RIDLEY'S LINNET
### *Canongate*, 1791.

ALAS, poor bird! art thou no more?
What language can thy loss deplore,
Thou who wast wont to be caress'd,
Thy bed prepared, thy cage well dress'd,
Thy drink so limpid, seed so rare,
Provided by good Granums care.
No more thou'lt hail the rising day,
No more thou'lt chirp, or hop, or play,
Or eye the family askance
At Johnny's song, or Betsy's dance.
Yet, ah! how blest thy little span,
Compared with that of hapless man!
Pleased to the last, thou hopp'd and sung,
No cares thy little bosom wrung;
No retrospect of evil past,
Anticipation's withering blast,
Malice' sharp tooth, or Envy's sting,
E'er hush'd thy song, or shrunk thy wing.
These demons were to thee unknown,
They haunt superior man alone.
Perhaps thy gentle spirit's lent
To inform some little, straggling ant;
Or in a bee, midst fragrant bowers,
Extracting sweets from blushing flowers;
Or, borne aloft o'er hill and dale,
Sings out in some sweet nightingale.
Where'er thou art, sweet bird, farewell!
In peace and safety may'st thou dwell;
Whilst I thy praises will rehearse,
And save thy memory in my verse.

## ANSWER TO MRS SAVILLE'S QUERY—
### "TO LOVE CAN ANYTHING BE A LABOUR?"

To mutual love nought can a labour be,
Where all is peace, and joy, and harmony.
Love unrequited labour all must prove,

Since Nature whispers, "Give me love for love."
Our kind exertions, whatsoe'er they cost,
Oh, may we never find Love's labour lost!

## ON LOVE AND FRIENDSHIP

TALK not of Love! it gives me pain—
For Love has been my foe:
He bound me in an iron chain!
And plunged me deep in wo!

But Friendship's pure and lasting joys
My heart was formed to prove—
The worthy object be of those,
But never talk of Love.

The "Hand of Friendship" I accept—
May Honour be our guard,
*Virtue* our intercourse direct,
Her smiles our dear reward.

Your thought, if Love must harbour there,
Conceal it in that thought,
Nor cause me from my bosom tear
The very friend I sought.

## TO MR ARCHIBALD MENZIES
*Canongate, 1791.*

MY dear and ever much respected friend,
Will you to-night a select few attend?
To see old Shakespeare's Hamlet tread the stage,
Hear the pale Ghost the Queen's sad doom presage;
Mourn o'er Ophelia's lost, distracted state,
Admire the Prince midst wild confusion great;
At each fine stroke throughout the churchyard scene,
Own that Immortal Shakespeare must remain.

## TO MISS AIKEN
EXTEMPORE
*Canongate, 1791.*

WHAT we feel our bosom doing,
When upon the brink of ruin,
Is the name of her I love,—
Shield her all ye powers above!

# APPENDIX V

## ~

### THREE 'MISSING' LETTERS FROM BURNS TO CLARINDA

Two of these letters were no great loss until their rediscovery. But the letter in which Burns shows himself to be guilty of bad faith, both to Clarinda and Jean Armour, is a crucial text with much to tell us about his cynical vacillation in conducting his affairs.

Weden noon: [*January 16th 1788*]

CLARINDA,—Your letter found me writing to you.—I read ours two or three times by way of welcome: by and by, I shall it more justice.— Friday evening, about eight, expect me.—If I can't walk all the way, I'll take a chair to Nicolson's square, or so; and walk the rest.—You talk of vanity; in mercy remember me, when you praise my letter-writing talents so extravagantly.—Inured to flattery as I have been for some time past, I am not proof against the applauses of one whom I love dearer, and whose judgement I esteem more, than I do all the world beside.—I forget the chairman waits—God bless you! Remember

SYLVANDER

[*Mossgiel, February 23rd 1788*]

I have just now, My ever dearest Madam, delivered your kind present to my sweet, little Bobbie; who I find a very fine fellow.—Your letter was waiting me.—Your interview with Mr K—— opens a wound, ill-closed, in my breast: not that I think his friendship of so much consequence to you, but because you set such a value on it.—Now for a little news that will please you.—I, this morning as I came home, called for a certain woman.—I am disgusted with her; I cannot endure her! I, while my heart smote me for the prophanity, tried to compare her with my Clarinda: 'twas setting the expiring glimmer of a farthing taper beside the cloudless glory of the meridian sun.—Here was tasteless insipidity, vulgarity of soul, and mercenary fawning; there, polished good sense, heaven-born genius, and the most generous, the most delicate, the most tender Passion.—I have done with her, and she with me.—

\*    \*    \*    \*    \*    \*    \*    \*    \*    \*    \*

I set off tomorrow for Dumfriesshire.—'Tis merely out of Compliment to Mr Miller, for I know the Excise must be my lot.—I will write you from Dumfries, if these horrid postages don't frighten me.—

> Whatever place, whatever land I see,
> My heart, untravell'd, fondly turns to thee:
> Still to "Clarinda" turns with ceaseless pain:
> And drags, at each remove, a lengthen'd chain!

I just stay to write you a few lines before I go to call on my friend, Mr Gavin Hamilton.—I hate myself as an unworthy sinner, because these interviews of old, dear friends make me for half a moment almost forget Clarinda.—Remember tomorrow evening at eight o'clock: I shall be with the Father of mercies, at that hour, on your account.—Farewell! if the post goes not tonight, I'll finish the other page tomorrow morning.—

SYLVANDER

[*Ellisland, February 1790*]

...in health. I do not rate the fatigue a farthing.—This labourious life secures me independance, a blessing which you know few people prize higher than I.

I could not answer your last letter but one when you in so many words tell a man that "you look on his letters with a smile of contempt", in what language Madam, can he answer you? Though I were conscious that I had acted wrong—and I am conscious that I have acted wrong—yet I would not be bullied into repentance but your last letter quite disarmed me—Determined as you...

# APPENDIX VI

## THE MONODY, EPITAPH AND EPIGRAM FROM LETTER LXIX

### Monody
#### On a Lady Famed for Her Caprice

How cold is that bosom which Folly once fired!
How pale is that cheek where the rouge lately glisten'd!
How silent that tongue which the echoes oft tired!
How dull is that ear which to flatt'ry so listen'd!

If sorrow and anguish their exit await,
From friendship and dearest affection remov'd;
How doubly severer, Maria, thy fate,
Thou diedst unwept, as thou livedst unlov'd.

Loves, Graces, and Virtues, I call not on you;
So shy, grave, and distant, ye shed not a tear:
But come, all ye offspring of Folly so true,
And flowers let us cull for Maria's cold bier.

We'll search through the garden for each silly flower,
We'll roam thro' the forest for each idle weed;
But chiefly the nettle, so typical, shower
For none e'er approached her but rued the rash deed.

We'll sculpture the marble, we'll measure the lay;
Here Vanity strums on her Idiot lyre;
There keen Indignation shall dart on his prey,
Which spurning Contempt shall redeem from his ire.

### The Epitaph

Here lies, now a prey to insulting neglect.
What once was a butterfly, gay in life's beam:
Want only of wisdom denied her respect,
Want only of goodness denied her esteem.

EPIGRAM
PINNED TO MRS WALTER RIDDELL'S CARRIAGE
If you rattle along like your Mistress's tongue,
  Your speed will outrival the dart;
But a fly for your load, you'll break down on the road,
  If your stuff be as rotten's her heart.

# NOTES

*The letters should be read headlong and with empathy. Footnotes would impede the narrative and emotional flow. Such endnotes as I provide are intended to introduce the offstage dramatis personae to contemporary readers. Burns and Clarinda quote copiously from Pope, Addison, Young, Milton, Shakespeare and many others. Those allusions can be identified from the comprehensive footnotes in Roy and Mackay. The notes here lean heavily and gratefully on Maurice Lindsay's* Burns Encyclopedia, *an endlessly useful resource.*

1   Miss Erskine Nimmo, an older friend of Clarinda, lived near her in Alison Square. She was a friend, too, of Peggy Chalmers, to whom Burns had proposed in this romantically crowded period of his life. Relations cooled, to Clarinda's dismay, because of the affair with Burns.

2   Alexander ('Lang Sandy', on account of his height and leanness) Wood (1725-1807), recommended Burns for the Excise job he sought and was the first man in Edinburgh to own an umbrella.

3   Jane Duchess of Gordon (1746-1812), a 'wild child' whose aplomb as a hostess made her the social arbiter of fashionable society. Painted by Reynolds, she was the beautiful, much-gossiped-about wife of the Duke of Gordon. Burns wrote to newspapers to defend her reputation. She was eventually ostracised and died in London.

4   Last stanza of an anonymous lyric in Allan Ramsay's influential *Tea Table Miscellany*.

5   Almost certainly 'On The Death Of Lord President Dundas'.

6   Dr James Gregory (1753-1821), the disputatious Professor of Medicine and grandson of the mathematician of the same name. He gave a copy of Cicero to Burns.

7   Bishop Geddes (1735-99). Dr John Geddes got the Scots Colleges at Valladolid and elsewhere in Europe to subscribe to the Edinburgh Edition and his annotated copy is known as the *Geddes Burns*.

8   James Johnson's collection of songs, of which, in effect, Burns was editor. In general, Johnson used the folk tunes Burns had composed to and specified rather than preferring or commissioning more 'classical' melodies, as George Thomson tended to in his *Select Airs*.

9   The celebrated Autobiographical Letter to the Glaswegian doctor who was to witness the French rising of 1792, and who urged Burns to write in English along the lines of Thomson's *Seasons*.

10  We too can only guess. By 1788, several contenders had emerged. The poet certainly felt guilty about his prevarication over and mistreatment of 'Highland Mary', whom he seems to have jilted after promising her a new life in Jamaica. Letter XVII makes clear his feelings for Peggy Chalmers.

11  Burns wrote several songs for Margaret Chalmers of Kirkcudbright (1763-1843), his muse and confidante, and Clarinda thought her a highly suitable wife for the poet. Her letters to him have disappeared.

12  James Elphinston(e) (1721-1809), was a friend of Dr Johnson. Carlyle called the London boarding school he ran a 'Jacobite seminary'. Both Burns and Johnson mocked his versions of Martial.

13  The traditional parting song, 'Gude night, and joy be wi' you a'', which Burns' own 'Auld Lang Syne' was largely and unintentionally to displace.

14  From Pope's *Eloisa to Abelard*, with the genders transposed.

15  Jenny Clow, a good soul indeed: she was to bear Burns a child. He was willing to take in her son, but Clarinda's servant would not part with the baby. Clarinda would subsequently write to notify him of her death. Burns treated Meg Cameron, another girl from the 'lower orders' who bore him a child in Edinburgh, much worse.

16  Robert Ainslie (1766-1838), the son of Lord Douglas' steward in Berwickshire, was a 'fun-loving' law student in Edinburgh. He accompanied Burns on his Borders tour of March 1787. In time his fondness for wine, women and song was replaced by religion.

17  '...Miss Nimmo's friend Mrs Stewart.'

18  A splendidly splenetic poem ('Here Stewarts once in triumph reign'd...'), vilifying the Hanoverians as an 'idiot race'; not Burns' first, nor his last entry into political controversy.

19  Mr Kemp became the Reverend Dr John Kemp (1744-1805), and acquired a Harvard doctorate in 1793. Thrice married, he was himself cited in divorce proceedings as the over-familiar confessor to Lady Colquhoun of Luss: only death saved him from disgrace.

20  Lord William Craig (1745-1813). As well as being a judge, Clarinda's cousin wrote (execrable) poetry and thus his jealousy of Burns was twofold.

21  Clarinda wishes to suppress Burns' anti-clericalism, which was never blasphemous nor irreverent.

22  A pretty decent pass at Standard Habbie, or the Burns stanza, with its trademark rhythmic pulling up short.

23  A songwriter, at her best to rival (because influenced by) Burns. Like Marion Angus and Helen Cruikshank after her, privilege did not prevent empathy with ordinary 'folk'.

24  It is not clear whether Kemp or Craig wrote the letter in question.

25  Craig and Kemp, both (almost literally) singing from the same hymn sheet, and both keen to see the back of Burns.

26  Clarinda's gift of baby clothes—shirts—for Burns' latest child.

27  Burns is affecting to be not worth the price of a letter—at that time the recipient paid the postage.

28  Alexander Pattison, a Paisley manufacturer, emigrated to America. Here he is

siding with Burns theologically in the liberal cause versus Kemp. Because he took and sold on several copies of the Edinburgh Edition, Burns called him the 'bookseller'.

29 Robert Graham of Fintry (in Forfarshire)(1749-1815), Commissioner of the Scottish Board of the Excise, was at Blair Castle when Burns visited the Duke of Atholl on his Highland tour. Burns backed up his letters with heroic couplets: 'I know my need, I know thy giving hand / I tax thy friendship at thy command'.

30 William Creech (1745-1815), the printer of the Edinburgh Edition, went on to become Provost. Burns' initial enthusiasm for him vanished amidst dithering, editorial sloppiness and bad faith over money.

31 Maria Ridell (1772-1808) was one of those high-born ladies with whom Burns felt able to correspond on very intimate terms. A hiatus in his relationship with Mrs Riddell was caused by Burns' conduct during the infamous re-enactment of the Rape of the Sabine Women at Friar's Carse near Dumfries. Always easily made drunk, the poet was goaded into having too much by the rich young men in Mrs Riddell's circle. Each was to 'charge', falling upon the prey of his choice after the ladies had withdrawn. Burns was egged on to go first, and this he did. None of the others followed. Burns caused outrage and was humiliated. His letter of repentance the next morning is a masterpiece of hungover remorse. Maria Riddell forgave him somewhat, but only very slowly. One of Burns' last and most poignant letters talks of seeing her in the next world.